THE SUM OF ALL
SPIRITUAL PATHS

Orest Stocco

THE SUM OF ALL SPIRITUAL PATHS

ISBN 978-1-926442-02-0

Edited by Penny Lynn Cates

Cover Design by Penny Lynn Cates

Letters to Padre Pio

Volume 2

*"Learn to love what you do, and do what you love;
that's the sum of all spiritual paths that will take you
to the Heart of God and happiness"*

Padre Pio

A GENTLE WORD

Our own life is the way, the path to one's true self. This is a simple truth, but it takes a long time to penetrate the mystery of this simple truth; perhaps a lifetime.

I awakened to my way early in life, thanks to a teaching brought to the western world by a remarkable man called Gurdjieff; a teaching of self-transformation that drew upon the same well of ancient wisdom that Jesus drank from, which is why Gurdjieff called his teaching "esoteric Christianity."

I was born Roman Catholic, but I left the Church at an early age in search of a path better suited to my spiritual needs. Life being the way of all ways, it follows that no spiritual path is more valid than another; they are all separate spokes of the same wheel of life. This is why the Sufis say that there are as many paths to God as there are souls of man, and why St. Padre Pio said to me, "Life is a journey of the self."

Padre Pio is a Roman Catholic saint, and I met him through a woman who has the gift of channeling the Ascended Master. I didn't know St. Padre Pio was an Ascended Master until I had several spiritual healing sessions with him; but it became obvious to me by how he responded to my troubled soul that he was more than a Christian saint, because he spoke from a consciousness of all knowing and seeing that inspired total confidence. My novel *Healing with Padre Pio* was based upon my ten spiritual healing sessions with him, but because I so enjoyed our special connection I decided to write him a letter whenever I felt a need to pour my heart out to the Ascended Master; hence my first volume *Letters to Padre Pio*.

I enjoy letter writing; and I especially enjoy reading books of private letters. I'm currently reading *Selected Letters of C. G. Jung, 1909-1961* and *Ernest Hemingway: Selected Letters 1917-1961* for my new book *The Lion that Swallowed Hemingway*, a literary memoir that brings my calling to become a writer and my calling to become a seeker into one life path of creative writing.

There's something about writing a personal letter that cannot be captured by any other form of writing, and it's a shame that letter writing is fast fading to the immediacy of social media, like email and Twitter; but I persist in writing letters.

Something magical happens when one writes a personal letter. The act of writing to another soul connects them in a special way that transcends both parties, as though a third party enters into the picture; and it's because of this third party that I relish writing to Ascended Master St. Padre Pio.

It took years to figure out who or what this third party was, but it finally dawned on me that it was the omniscient guiding force of life; and I say this because after years of writing I came to see that the gems of wisdom that flow out of the creative process can come from nowhere else but some divine agency, and writing personal letters is one of the most effective ways to tap into the precious wisdom of this agency.

That's why I love writing letters to St. Padre Pio. I am doubly blessed, because being an Ascended Master he is one with this divine agency, and when I write him to address a certain concern my creative unconscious flows through me with such fluidity that I'm often amazed by what comes through.

Sometimes I can feel St. Padre Pio's presence in my thoughts, and I just let him speak for himself. I have several letters in which we simply dialogue. Of course, I could never prove that it was St. Padre Pio that I dialogued with just as Neale Donald Walsh cannot prove that he had conversations with God, but that's of no importance to me; what is important is the healing goodness that I get from my letters of the heart.

Because St. Padre Pio is an Ascended Spiritual Master, he transcends the rigid parameters of his Roman Catholic faith; so the wisdom that comes through speaks not only to me, but to the whole world. For this reason I wish to share my letters to Padre Pio; because, as he said, "I can be of more use to you in heaven than I have been on earth. I belong to everyone; everyone will say Padre Pio is mine. I can refuse no one, since the Good Lord has never refused my humble request," and I feel that in some small measure my letters will assist him in his mission.

As personal as my letters may be they are a testament of my path, which I forged out of all the spiritual teachings that I have studied; and I can only hope that what comes through will have a healing effect upon the anguished soul of our troubled world. I wrote these letters as the spirit moved me, in the realization that our own life is the sum of all spiritual paths, and in the certain knowledge that if we are true to ourselves we will find our own way to wholeness and happiness, which is our divine heritage; and I invite you to join me in my new epistolary journey.

Orest Stocco,
Bluewater, Georgian Bay
June 2, 2014

LETTERS

1. *The Day Before Prophecy Day*

Wednesday, December 20, 2012

Dear Padre,

Tomorrow is the Mayan December 21st 2012 prophecy day that everyone is anxiously waiting for. You told me in one of my spiritual healing sessions with the lady who channeled you for my book *Healing with Padre Pio* that it would be a smooth shift in consciousness and that there was nothing to worry about. I asked about this because of all the gloom and doom that attended the Mayan prophecy, and I was curious to see what answer you would give from your place of all knowing and seeing.

You didn't elaborate on this shift in world consciousness, but I found out from another source during my research for another book that I'm working on that December 21st, 2012 is the threshold date when the negative forces of the world are going to be slightly overtaken by the positive forces of the world, and from this date on the positive forces of the world will have an edge over the negative forces; hence, things will begin to gradually improve in the world because we won't be as strongly inclined to be negative.

At the risk of revealing something that perhaps shouldn't be revealed, when I received my Fifth Initiation in my spiritual path I experienced something that will shed light on this shift in world consciousness.

The Fifth Initiation in my path is an initiation into the Soul Plane of Consciousness, the first of the spiritual worlds of God above the material worlds of the Mental, Causal, Astral, and Physical Planes; and upon receiving my Fifth Initiation I felt a shift in polarity: I was being pulled upward and not downward as I was before my initiation into the Soul Plane.

It was a subtle but still noticeable shift in polarity, and I *knew* because I felt that the negative forces of life no longer had the same hold on me. This is what I believe is going to happen on prophecy day tomorrow: there is going to be a shift in the polarity of world consciousness from the negative to the positive. It won't be a dramatic shift, but it will be powerful enough to start shifting the focus of humanity's attention from self-serving ego (our lower self) to Soul (our higher self).

You did tell me that the world was being assisted by higher beings on the Other Side to make this shift in consciousness. They (and I assume this means you also) have been infusing the world with spiritual energy to raise the consciousness of the world; and on December 21, 2012 the world will reach the threshold and the shift in polarity from the negative to the positive forces will occur, thereby changing the course of world history. And this opens up the question of the split of Planet Earth into two worlds; one world going into the Fifth Dimension, and the other remaining in the lower worlds. And those who are ready will go with the new Earth, and those who aren't ready will stay with the old Earth.

This information was released by Dolores Cannon, the past-life regression hypnotherapist who gets her information from the same place that Edgar Cayce got his (the Universal Mind); but this is too much for me to wrap my head around, so I'm going to leave it until I read a few more of her books.

I've read two of her books (*Jesus and the Essenes*, and *They Walked with Jesus*), and I loved them. They resonated, because I had a past life as an Essene during the time of Jesus; but that's another story. The point I want to explore with you, starting with this letter, is this shift in consciousness from the negative to the positive.

As you know, I've been doing research on Carl Jung for my new book, and I've been listening to lectures online on Jung's *Red Book* (*Liber Novus*), which I've just ordered from Amazon (I was hoping it would be in for Christmas, but its due arrival date is December 28), and I was so engaged in Jung's vision experience (which he later called his "confrontation with the unconscious") that my Muse gave me the title of a new book to write—*The Beauty of Suffering, Reflections on Jung's Red Book.*

I can't wait to delve into *The Red Book* so I can build my foundation for my new book (the title comes from what Jesus told Jung in his vision of Soul's natural individuation through life: "I bring you the beauty of suffering"), because I know that this title will reflect the genius of Jung's hermeneutics of the *individuation process*—which you realized by living *la via di sofferenza* (the way of suffering), and I realized by living the way according to Gurdjieff and the sayings of Jesus.

I lived my own gnostic path, if you will; and by this I mean the Way of the Eternal, which is the way of spiritual wisdom garnered from every walk of life. Anyway, Padre; I just wanted to begin a new series of letters because I want to stay connected with the creative life stream. I completed my final edit of *Letters to Padre Pio* yesterday, and I was nudged to begin another volume; so, if I may, would you please accompany me on another epistolary journey to wherever Spirit wishes to take us?

In Spirit, your faithful companion,
Orest

2. *What Now Brown Cow?*

Sunday, December 23, 2012

Dear Padre,

Prophecy Day has come and gone. We are two days into the shift in world consciousness and I'm not sure I notice the difference. The days seem to be unfolding like before, so if there is a difference (which I believe there is because I don't doubt what you told me) I just haven't noticed it yet. Perhaps it's too subtle for me to notice at the moment, or I have not yet caught the momentum of the shift.

I've been thinking of our next project together. I know we won't begin our next project for a year or so yet because I have to write two books before we do (*The Summoning of Noman, The True Story of My Parallel Life*; and *The Beauty of Suffering, Reflections of Jung's Red Book*), but my Muse did give me the working title of our next project: *Dialogues with St. Padre Pio*. What do you think?

I mentioned in my last spiritual healing session with you that I felt my entry point into our next project was going to be the *Book of Ecclesiastes*, and I have to tell you that nothing seems to have changed this feeling. The Preacher asks the question, "What profit hath a man of all his labor which he taketh under the sun?" after telling us that all is vanity; and then he goes on to tell us to just go out and live our life and obey the commandments of God. I have caught the gnostic wisdom of *Ecclesiastes*, and I can't wait to dialogue with you on the natural process of spiritual individuation—which gives me the theme of today's letter: what now brown cow?

Before prophecy day and after prophecy day, the entry point into the kingdom of heaven (to use Christ's phrase for the Way) was and is our very own life; which is why Jesus said that the kingdom of heaven was within. So what does the brown cow do now? We do what we've always been doing, but instead of living our life with unconscious awareness of our spiritual purpose in life we can now live our bovine little life with *conscious intent*—i. e., with the realization that the purpose of life, as you told me in one of our sessions, is all about GROWTH and UNDERSTANDING— only now we can grow in understanding with a *conscious intent*, which changes the flavor of our life significantly!

This is the difference between living our life with meaningful purpose and not living it with meaningful purpose. Jung spent his life trying to conceptualize his understanding of the individuation process of the unconscious, and he came to the conclusion that as long as we are unconscious of our own process of individuation we will always be floating on a sea of paradoxical meaningless purpose; but the moment we bridge the chasm between our outer and inner self we will connect with our own process of individuation and live life with a *conscious intent* that gives our life meaningful purpose.

This is why I can't wait to read Jung's *Red Book*, which he declares to be the foundation of his psychology of individuation. My copy should arrive next week, due date December 28; and I know that once I get into it I won't be able to put it down because the lectures that I heard on *The Red Book* have done nothing but enhance my feelings of affinity with Carl Jung—as though we are initiates of the same teaching of the Way, which he calls the *process of individuation* and I call the Way of the Eternal.

Incidentally Padre, last night I had a dream which suggests that this affinity I have with Carl Jung is not wishful thinking or a figment of my imagination. I was dining in a very private restaurant on the shores of a lake at the foot of Alpine-like mountains—a very Swiss-like setting. Jung lived on the shores of Lake Zurich, and he often gave private lectures at a friend's house in Ascona on the shores of Lake Maggiore. The qualifications for membership into this private gathering of speakers was a dedicated commitment to seek out life's purpose (as Jung had done, and as I have done) and then share it with the world.

That's why I wrote *Healing with Padre Pio*, to share my gnostic wisdom with the world; and that's what I did with my new novel *Jesus Wears Dockers, The Gospel Conspiracy Story*. I might add that I probably wouldn't publish this novel had you not encouraged me to get it out there; so, thank you Padre.

In Spirit, I remain
Your happy companion,
Orest

3. *It's All a Question of Being*

Tuesday, December 26, 2012

Dear Padre

I didn't expect to get them before Christmas, but the new books that I ordered from Amazon were delivered to my front door on the 24th, and I felt like a kid who had just received the Christmas present he had been praying for!

The books were: *Jung and the Lost Gospels*, by Stephan A. Hoeller; Jung's *Mysterium Coniunctionis*; *The Secret of the Golden Flower* (A Chinese Book of Life), with a commentary by C. G. Jung; *The Gnostic Bible*; and *Meister Eckhart.*

I opened the box, unwrapped the books from their plastic wrap, perused them all quickly, and then read snippets of each starting with *The Secret of the Golden Flower* and ending with Jung's ponderous tome *Mysterium Coniunctionis*; and then I dove into *The Secret of the Golden Flower* because this was the book that moved Jung enough to stop working on his *Red Book* because he had found the proof he was looking for in the ancient Chinese text that the translator Richard Wilhelm had asked him to write a commentary for—and of course I went to the back of the book and read Jung's commentary first!

Well Padre, I've almost completely read *The Secret of the Golden Flower* and a good chunk of *Jung and the Lost Gospels,* and I came to a conclusion that I have not been able to embrace for a long time now. I've know this for years, but as I read *The Secret of the Golden Flower* the truth was forced upon me and it filled me with sadness.

I didn't want to say goodbye to the longing that searching for the Way gave me, but I knew deep inside that because I had found the Way I had to let go of my desire to hold onto that feeling of excitement that looking for the Way gave me and just *be* the Way!

God, I can't begin to explain how excited I would get whenever the scent of the Way brought me closer to the Way with each new discovery that I made, which all started with P. D. Ouspensky's book *In Search of the Miraculous* back in university where the scent had taken me when I came back from France where I had gone to begin my quest for the Way!

Now, just because I found the Way doesn't mean that I am in total consciousness of the Way (as you are, which is why you could relate to me as you did—with a total awareness of my life that convinced me you spoke from a place of all knowing); so I do get excited whenever I come upon another book that will expand my horizons on the Way—which is precisely what happened when I was working on my novel *Healing with Padre Pio.*

I came upon books by pure chance (chance, alright!) that sent me into spasms of pure joy—like coming across the book *90 Minutes in Heaven* by chance in the Bayfield Mall in Barrie, or the book that was brought right to my front door *(The Only Planet of Choice)*, and of course the book that you recommended I read *(Love without End, Jesus Speaks)*; but I need not expound upon how Divine Spirit guided me during the writing of *Healing with Padre Pio* because it's all there in my novel.

I just don't want to create the wrong impression that just because I found the Way doesn't mean I have lost interest in how other people look for the Way; and it especially excites me when I read a book of someone finding the Way—like *The Music Lesson*, by Victor L. Wooten; or *The Inspired Heart*, by Jerry Wennstrom. The point I want to make is that having found the Way I now must *be* the Way; because that's what the Way demands of me. But like I said, I've been avoiding accepting this responsibility—until it was forced upon me as I read *The Secret of the Golden Flower.*

It's not as simple as I'm making it out. I do live the Way, so I *am* my way; because when one finds the Way he finds it according to his own individual path—whatever that path may be. You, for example, found the Way as you lived *la via di sofferenza*. The way of Christ's suffering was your way; so you *were* the Way. Music was Victor L. Wootan's path to the Way, and he lives the Way of music. Art was Jerry Wenstrom's way, but it didn't connect him with the Way on the deep level that he needed; so he abandoned his art and made of his own life the path to the Way, which he found. So his life *is* his Way. And my life *is* my Way; but I kept this realization at arm's length because I didn't want to acknowledge the full consciousness of what it means for one's own life to *be* the Way. But this is what reading *The Secret of the Golden Flower* forced upon me!

There; I finally said it! I own my own truth now, as the expression goes; and I have no more excuses to not trust my own truth and just go with it! Which means that I don't have to wait to read all those books I felt I should read (I'm going to be ordering another ten or so books for my research on Jung) to get back into my own book *The Summoning of Noman* which I've been putting off, using the excuse that I had to read all these books before I could complete my book; so, as terrified as I was about diving back into my book I have the realization now that I can trust in my consciousness of the Way to complete my book without the fear of not doing it justice. In a word, Padre; I *am* my own Way, and it's all a question of *being* now!

In Spirit, your resolved companion,
Orest

4. *Liber Novus*

Dear Padre,

I have some exciting news to share. As you know, I've been doing extensive research on C. G. Jung (I've read half a dozen biographies already, plus a number of other related books—i. e., on Gnosticism; as well as reading Jung's works), and the day before Christmas all the books but one that I had ordered from Amazon arrived, which I dove into immediately; but today Jung's *Liber Novus* (*The Red Book)* arrived at my front door just as I was listening to an online lecture by Stephan A. Hoeller: *Gnosticism: A New Light on the Ancient Tradition of Inner Knowing.* Coincidence or what?

Jung's *Liber Novus* is a modern day Gnostic gospel because it's the record of his initiation into Gnosis—and I have capitalized the word Gnosis because for me Gnosis and the Way are one and the same. In effect, Jung's unbelievable encounter with the unconscious initiated him into the mysteries of the Way; which he ends up calling the *process of individuation* because that definition best fits his historical worldview.

I wanted to dive right into it, but I only perused the book and then listened to the last ten minutes of

Hoeller's lecture; and then I read the table of contents and Preface to *A Reader's Edition*, and then the Preface by Editor Sonu Shamdasani.

I wanted to dive into *Liber Novus*, but I was too excited and instead went for a walk around Stocco Circle (our street); and when I came back I shoveled the snow off the back deck because we have new furniture being delivered this morning and we have to take the old furniture out, so we're going to keep it on our back deck and have it hauled away later. And then I came upstairs to write you a letter, because I simply had to share what all of my reading on Jung has done to me—which became so apparent as I held *The Red Book, Liber Novus, A Reader's Edition* in my hand that I could no longer deny my humbling experience.

Padre, you did a number on me with my spiritual healing sessions; you slew my vanity with your devastating humility (which I addressed in *Healing with Padre Pio*); but that was the vanity of my spiritual conceit. All of my research on C. G. Jung has finally slain the vanity of my intellectual conceit, and I feel absolutely ridiculous now!

My God, I cannot believe the depths of my intellectual conceit! The more I read of Jung and his works, the more humbling his prodigious mind made me feel; and as I held *Liber Novus* in my hands today I could not stop the grace of his gnosis from completely vaporizing the vanity of my intellectual conceit! Just when you think you're home free, along comes another killer blow to your ego; but what a wonderful relief!

I have to share something else with you, Padre. Before going for my walk I decided to do that little technique I do every so often—the one where I open a book at random just to see what the omniscient guiding force of life has to tell me; and I opened *Liber Novus* at random ready to point my finger to a paragraph hoping for a little sage piece of wisdom from Carl Jung's own mouth, and the book opened to a blank page with the words *Liber Primus* (which means First Book)!

So, Padre; what's Divine Spirit telling me? That this is the entry point into the first book of my own initiation experience into Gnosis—because I did get the insight to write a book on Jung's *Liber Novus*, with the title ready-made: *The Beauty of Suffering: Reflections on Jung's Red Book*? This insight came to me after I listened to Dr. Lance Owens series of lectures on *The Red Book*. I was so inspired by Jung's *Red Book* that I knew I would have to reveal my own experiences that awakened me to Gnosis!

A new world has opened up to me, Padre. You did tell me that I had transcended my own voice, as well as the voice of my spiritual community; so is this the voice that wants to be heard now in *The Beauty of Suffering*?

I hope so, because I can't wait to write it. But I have a long way to go before I write this one. I have to finish *The Summoning of Noman* first, which will take all winter and most of the spring; and then hopefully I can start *The Beauty of Suffering*. But right now I'm going to dive into Jung's *Liber Novus*; so if you'll pardon me, I'm going to say goodbye for now. Until the next time...

I remain,
A very happy camper,
Orest

5. *First Impressions of Liber Novus*

Tuesday, January 1, 2013

Dear Padre,

I finished reading *Liber Novus* at 8:35 this morning, New Year's Day, 2013. I received the book on the 28th of December, and in less than one week I managed to complete this ponderous, but absolutely fascinating tome of 582 pages. I did most of my reading in our family room in front of a cozy fire, and I relished every moment of Jung's unbelievable journey! Okay, Padre; what are my first impressions of *Liber Novus*?

Without thinking, I'm just going to let my inner self reveal how I feel. First, I loved the challenge of reading Jung's private account of his confrontation with the unconscious because I couldn't wait to compare his confrontation with mine; and I wasn't disappointed. His account is so rich in detail, so mesmerizing in scholarly brilliance and historical perspective, and so glaring in its audacity that I JUST LOVED IT!

Second, I couldn't wait to see what was around the next bend. Each page offered something new and fascinating confirmation of my own confrontation with the unconscious, and I read *Liber Novus* like a thrilling mystery novel!

What I found amazing as I read Jung's account of his visions and fantasies was his incredible ability to treat his inner-worldly experience as an extension of his normal daily life, which gave remarkable credibility to the surreal reality of his soul travels into the depths of the collective unconscious; and once I adjusted to the logic of his experiences I realized that this whole account was an allegory of Soul's journey through life—specifically, Jung's individuating Soul self!

It took a while to see it (perhaps at midpoint of the book), but once I saw it something clicked and the whole book made sense to me on the allegorical level: I suddenly realized that the world of the collective unconscious is peopled by the archetypal realities of life—both material and spiritual life. Once I realized that the people he met in his visions and fantasies were not symbols but actual realities, I began to understand Jung's persistent claims that the psyche is a reality in its own right!

Suddenly Jung's whole psychology of the unconscious took on new meaning, and I can't wait to reread his works (those that I have read; I'm going to order more of his works as soon as I've gobbled up the books that just came in) because now I know that his whole psychology was born of his experience in *Liber Novus* and I will be able to discern his exoteric articulation of his esoteric experience much more easily!

And, I have to tell you Padre; once I finished reading *Liber Novus* this morning in front of the cozy fire I knew that I just had to write my book *The Beauty of Suffering*—because Jung's personal confrontation with the unconscious gives me the perfect historical confirmation for my own remarkable journey through the depths of my own soul; which is why my Muse gave me the subtitle to my book: *Reflections of Jung's Red Book.*

Liber Novus is the most courageous book I have ever read. No wonder Jung did not want it published in his lifetime. In fact, it took fifty years before his family gave permission to release it; and there is a whole story in that, which Sonu Shamdasani, the editor of *Liber Novus*, explains in his introduction.

One thing came to me this morning as I reflected on *Liber Novus* that I have to share with you, Padre: Jung's confrontation with the unconscious—all those mythical people and animals that he encountered in the deep—have led me to the very strong conviction that all those gods of Greek mythology were no less real! And I have no doubt that they manifested to the ancient Greeks as the mythical figures in Jung's visions and fantasies manifested to him. Which lends a whole new perspective on the mythologies of the world!

But that's too abstract and metaphysical for the world to buy into, so I won't bother pursuing it. Suffice to say that *Liber Novus* has made it possible for me to resume my work on *The Summoning of Noman*, which will prepare me for *The Beauty of Suffering*! Bye for now, Padre...

Your refreshed companion,
Orest

19

6. *There Is Only Today*

Friday, January 4, 2013

Dear Padre,

It's not pressing on me, but I'm beginning to think the unthinkable; just fleeting thoughts, not enough to worry me, but enough to take notice. I'm talking about "time's winged chariot" that's beginning to draw near—my own death.

It took a lot to say it, but I've been thinking about my own death because of the books I have to get out before I die. The truth is, I can't wait to cross over to the Other Side; but I know I have to get out the books that I have already written, plus the ones that are pressing upon me to write—i. e., *The Summoning of Noman* and *The Beauty of Suffering*.

Penny is half way through her edit of *Jesus Wears Dockers, The Gospel Conspiracy Story*; so it should be ready to submit for a proof copy by the end of this month. Then we will read it once more, make our corrections, and it should be out by spring; and that will take a lot of pressure off me because this is the book you wanted me to publish.

I asked you why I was hesitant to publish this novel, and you said it was because I didn't want to go back there; meaning, the original source of my faith—Christianity. You said that I was avoiding it. Well, with the research I've been doing on Carl Jung's life and psychology I'm not hesitant any more. In fact I think I'm going to delve into *The Gnostic Bible* next to explore the esoteric side of Christianity. And I'm going to finish reading my books on St. John of the Cross and St. Teresa of Avila just to get a feel of the interior life as these Christian mystics lived it.

You were a Christian mystic, Padre; and I loved talking with you in my spiritual healing sessions. I loved your all-knowing and all seeing perspective. It was so refreshing to speak with someone who KNEW and did not have to work out an answer to whatever I asked. I never experienced that before; or, rather, I did but in small doses. With you, I had total confidence in your all-knowing perspective; but I didn't always agree with you. Which made for an interesting dialogue, as *Healing with Padre Pio* reveals.

Now I have a question for you. I'm going to write *The Summoning of Noman: The True Story of My Parallel Life*; but I want to know if I should do my next project with you before I take on my book *The Beauty of Suffering: Reflections on Jung's Red Book*, or whether I should write *The Beauty of Suffering* before I do my next book with you.

I'm not quite sure what I should do; but I feel that I would need your all-knowing and all seeing perspective to give me a firmer foundation for *The Beauty of Suffering*, because you lived the "beauty" of Christ's suffering, which you called your "glory." This way I would have my new book with you to draw upon

21

to give *The Beauty of Suffering* all the authenticity and credibility that it will deserve—because it might just be the book that spells out the unedited story of my own initiation into the secret way of life!

I still have time to think about this, but I thought I would put it to you so you can toss it over and let me know which way to go. I trust your judgment.

I can feel your presence now, and I can almost hear you telling me that it's time I got back to writing *The Summoning of Noman*. If I may, I'm going to dialogue with you: what's holding me back from working on it?

"*You hesitate because you feel you need more information; but you have all the information you need to get the story going. What more information you need will come to you in the process of writing it. This is how it works with you. Just do it.*"

"What about the question I just asked you? Should I do my next project with you after I write *The Summoning of Noman* in preparation for *The Beauty of Suffering*?"

"*I look forward to our next project. It will be very rewarding for both of us. It will happen, so do not fret. Just do what you have to do. And yes, I do believe that it will be necessary for your book The Beauty of Suffering. I love this title, by the way. It is very close to my heart.*"

"I know. That's why I thought it would be best to do our next book before I write *The Beauty of Suffering*. Good God, Padre; I do so love what Jung has done for the world with his remarkable contribution. Thank him for me over there, will you please?"

"He's very well aware of your work; and he says you're welcome."

"I still have my novel with him to rework, *The Waking Dream*; but I don't want to rework this until I am thoroughly versed on his life and psychology."

"He knows, and he's looking forward to assisting you on it now that you have fully grasped the principle of his teaching. He knew you weren't ready to send that book out as it was; that's why there were complications with it. But it will be rewritten, and it will be a wonderful novel that you will be proud of."

"I don't want to overdo this aspect of our relationship, but I have a feeling that this is leading to a new "Soul talk" book. Am I right?"

"More than a feeling. It is a certainty, but not yet. After you get a few more books out you will indulge yourself in this form of creative expression, and it will prove very enjoyable—not to mention informative. Enough for now."

"Thank you."

"You're welcome. Don't hesitate. Get back into your book. You will be more engaged in it than you ever dreamt because the way has been paved. All of your reading has given you the information and confidence you need to write that book. And write from the heart. Pour yourself into it. Just let your heart speak."

"I'll do the best I can."

"That's all anyone can ask of you. Live, love, and enjoy your life; and don't worry about tomorrow. Tomorrow never comes. There is only today."

"I hear you, Padre. Bye for now."

I am, in Spirit
Your thankful companion,
Orest

7. *Getting to the Core of My Being*

Saturday, January 12, 2013

Dear Padre,

Well, I did get back to writing *The Summoning of Noman*. I wrote Chapter Ten: "The Shadow Personality," and yesterday started Chapter Eleven: "A Whole New Look at Reincarnation," but I had to stop because the energy was so strong that I was much too anxious to continue. I was hoping to resume writing this morning, but I decided to write you a letter to let you know that something is happening to me. Maybe you can give me some insight to what's going on. It has to do with the heart.

You are an expert on the heart. Your love and compassion opened your heart to the world, and you are the most qualified to inform me. You gave me the advice in my last letter to write from the heart. "Just let your heart speak," you said, which I have begun to do; but this is having a peculiar effect on me: it is bringing me to the core, and the closer I get to the core of who I am, the stronger the pulse of life—and this frightens me.

I don't quite know how to express this, but I suspect that this is the source of artistic brilliance. I hesitate to use the word genius, but this would be appropriate considering what the great artists throughout the centuries have produced; and it had to come from somewhere, did it not? Well, I suspect it came from the core of their being.

The core of one's being is one with the Source; this is why the currents of energy are so powerful and why it frightened me yesterday as I felt myself approaching the core of my being and had to stop writing. But just what do I mean by the core of my being?

For the past few months I have been firming up my suspicion that the Now of one's life is the entry point (pathway would be a better word) to the Source; and by Source I mean that which is: God! Well Padre, all of my research into parallel worlds, depth psychology, Gnosticism and everything related to this fascinating world of spiritual mysteries, the more I am convinced that my personal relationship with the Way convinces me that the individual experience of one's life—be it what it may, preparing dinner, driving to work, watering one's plants, golfing or whatever—is the entry point to the Whole, to the core of one's being; and this frightens me. In a word, one's own life is the Way; that's why your advice was to live and enjoy my life.

This is why I've been nudged to read short stories lately. I've been going back to the short story because the short story is a moment of life frozen in time; a glimpse into the core of human nature—which is why the short story is such a powerful medium to give expression to the unfolding human condition.

Meaning: I've come to realize that no matter what path one seeks in life (and I have explored many), it all comes right down to the core of one's being—one's very own life; because the Now of one's life experiences is the God-given pathway into the core of one's being, and the Heart of God—LOVE!

This is the mystery, isn't it Padre? This is what you have been trying to teach me, the mystery of LOVE; isn't it? You have been trying to tell me that the more honest I am in my writing from the heart, the closer I will get to the core of my being—which is LOVE.

LOVE is who we are. This is what the world consciousness has finally come to realize today. This concept of LOVE being the *sine qua non* of existence is becoming the theme of today's spirituality, and your life is proof of this—*right?*

So that's why I had to stop writing yesterday. I was getting too close to the core of my being, and I couldn't take the energy. It was too much for me. Wow!

This is a big concept, and I will be exploring it in my books; probably starting with *The Summoning of Noman.* I think I'm ready to get back to work on my chapter now; so I thank you for listening to me. I got the message loud and clear; but this doesn't mean that I'm less anxious about writing to the core of my being. I have to approach this slowly, because the energy of LOVE can fry me to a crisp!

Hey, isn't that what I'm going to explore with my book *The Beauty of Suffering*? Isn't that what the theme of that book is going to be—LOVE?

LOVE is the beauty of suffering. This is the gift that Jesus gave to the world. This is what Jesus meant in the last line of Jung's *Liber Novus*, isn't it? God, I feel like my book has already been written. The mystery is gone now, and all I have to do is work out the details. Thanks a lot, Padre! Where's the challenge now?

I remain, your happy companion,
Orest

8. *Another Biography of Your Life, By an Atheist, No Less*

Saturday, February 9, 2013

Dear Padre,

It's been almost one month since I wrote you a letter and I feel inclined this morning to talk with you. I've been in a rather strange mood lately, ever since I found out that our neighbor is going to be taking an early retirement. He's going to put his house up for sale and move away. He has a young wife, from the Philippines, and it's going to be hard on her when they move. Penny has taken his young wife under her wing, and they are going to miss each other; but life goes on, and we have to live with the changes that come our way.

But I have to wonder though, because anyone we develop a friendship with eventually is taken from our life; and Penny and I end up alone. Not that we mind our aloneness, we love each other enough to withstand the blows of life (and there have been plenty); but we would like to have some graceful years before parting this world.

It's been a long haul, Padre. We've been through quite a bit, and I hope to God that the worst is behind us. We would love to see some of my books find their readers before I pass on, but I have the creeping suspicion that I am writing for posterity. I hope not, because I would love to have the satisfaction of seeing at least one of my books "make it," as the phrase goes.

We got *Jesus Wears Dockers, The Gospel Conspiracy Story* all proofed and out, and it is available on Kindle on Amazon and paperback on Lulu. It should be available in paperback on Amazon in a couple of months. I hope it finds its readers. Remember, this is the book that you wanted to see out there; well, it's out now. Hope you like it.

Speaking of books, I just read another biography of your life; *Padre Pio, Miracles and Politics in a Secular Age,* by Sergio Luzzatto. I first heard of this book last summer on the CBC radio show *Tapestry.* Sergio Luzzatto was being interviewed by Mary Hynes. His biography of your life had just won a prestigious award. I enjoyed the interview, despite the fact that Sergio was a self-confessed atheist (which I found rather ironic, given that your life was so Christ-centered); but the book proved to be quite informative. It gave me a good glimpse at the atmosphere and culture in which you evolved as a living saint, and I have to say Padre, you had to endure much more than the holy wounds of Jesus; didn't you?

What we don't have to do to realize our true self! I'm more than half finished writing my book *The Summoning of Noman,* and I have to confess that it's finding its own direction. I'm doing a lot of leaning upon the synchronistic principle to bring this book together, and it seems to be working; but I really don't know how much closer I am to understanding this concept of my parallel life. I feel I have a grasp, but not enough of a hold to give me a feeling of certainty. I hope by the time I finish it I will be sure.

I should mention Padre, because I think you nudged me to go ahead with this change in my life, that Penny and I purchased a juicer called Nutri-Bullet. This juicer mixes vegetables and fruits and nuts and seeds into nutritious drinks, and believe it or not in less than a week Penny and I have begun to feel the difference in our health. We would both like to lose some weight, and this seems to be a healthy way of doing it.

Now Padre, I would like to make a request. I hate to do this, but what the heck; I have your ear, so why not ask? I would love nothing more than to see our life (Penny and me) go gracefully into the night, with quiet dignity and sweet humility. Would you in your wisdom and sanctity help us realize this simple request?

Thank you,
Orest

9. *The More I Read, the Less I Know*

Tuesday, April 2, 2013

Dear Padre,

I'm in a strange place. Don't quite know how to describe it. I read so many books for my book *The Summoning of Noman, The True Story of My Parallel Life* that I had a startling epiphany. It came at me in a blinding flash of humbling despair: *the more I read, the less I know!* It stopped me in my tracks. I couldn't move. My mind froze.

I've been like this for a week or so now, and I can't wait for this mood—or whatever it is—to go away. It's playing upon my self-confidence. What to do?

Jump right in and do something. That's the answer. In the doing there is the joy of being; and in the joy of being despair has no place to show itself. But doesn't this suggest doing without thought? Some kind of surrender to the process?

It seems that this is how I always go into a new book that I am called to write; I just jump right in. And the more I proceed trusting the process, the more ground I seem to stand on; until I have enough ground to make a book. And that's a good feeling. Which I felt when I finished writing *The Summoning of Noman.* But now I feel the PCBs.

The PCBs are those nasty little demons that I have called post creative blues. They come whenever I bring a new book to closure. Well, whatever it is that I'm experiencing, I know that I have to start a new project to get myself out of this state; so, what now?

I'd love to start my next project with you, Padre; but I'm not quite ready yet to begin a new book with you. I do have the title, though. I want to call our next book *Padre Pio Speaks from Heaven*. What do you think of the title?

I told the woman who channeled you for *Healing with Padre Pio* that I would be contacting her sometime this summer, but I don't know when exactly. I still feel that I have a few more books to read before I engage in another dialogue with you. I want to be ready to receive the kind of information I'm hoping to get from you this time. I want to explore what you called "the inner workings of the universe."

I don't know if I will ever be ready for this information, but I have to go with my intuition; and I feel that I have to complete my reading on Jung and the dreaming process as it is being researched today by Robert Moss and others, because this is cutting edge knowledge, so when we do our project we can expand the horizon of understanding the inner workings of the universe a millimeter or two.

I suspect that it comes back to the NOW of our life. That all of this knowledge, however cutting edge it may be, adds up to a big fat zero with respect to the meaning and purpose of our life; because the only thing that matters in the end is how we choose to live our life. Knowledge is good to have, but wisdom on how to live our life is better; and by wisdom I mean the enlightened understanding of how to live our life so that we can grow into the person that we are meant to be.

Eureka! I just found my way out of my humbling despair! It's not what I know that will add another cubit to my stature, but what I do! As long as I do what I feel I am meant to do—in my case, write—than I am fulfilling my purpose in life!

I don't have to be intimidated by my awakened sense of abysmal ignorance, because there is no end to knowledge. It's a mug's game. Just do what I have to do and read what I feel I have to read for what I have to do, and let the universe unfold as it will; and maybe, just maybe, the inner workings of the universe will be revealed to me.

That's all for today, Padre. Until the next time,

I am, your companion in Spirit,
Orest

10. *Yesterday Was Not a Good Day*

Saturday, April 6, 2013

Dear Padre,

Yesterday Penny went to the bank to check out whether our tenant had made his deposit into our account. He owes us $2,100 for back rent. He promised he would make the deposit, but he hasn't. Penny needed that money to pay the installment taxes on our triplex and on our house here in Georgian Bay. Now she may have to draw on her savings because we are already making monthly drawings from my savings.

She feels that our tenant is going to stiff us. This put us into a funk yesterday, and last night we couldn't sleep. It felt like the walls were closing in on us, but I told her that we have choices. Our ship is not going to sink; it just may not sail where we would like it to sail. But it never does. Our life is choreographed from on high even though we may be captain of our own ship. It's a real mystery, but one which I've been trying to solve for a long time. I think this has to do with what you call "the inner workings of the universe."

Padre, in all honesty Penny and I are tired of the same old bullshit. We trust people, but not all people are trustworthy. Is this just another lesson in the unending journey of lessons that we have to learn in this relentless life?

"Pray, hope, and don't worry." That was your saying. I wish I could stop worrying. I don't know how. It's a habit that I picked up from my mother. Worrying was to her nature as the color of her eyes. I know that worrying doesn't solve anything. It only serves to drain us of our precious life force, but how to stop? That's the question.

I berate myself for not being better off today. I could have provided for Penny a lot better than I have, and I feel like such a fool for spending so much time on my quest and writing. It doesn't seem to amount to a hill of beans. But then, I wouldn't have met you for a spiritual healing, would I? Had I pursued financial security, I would have ended up like I did in my other lives—economically secure, but spiritually empty.

So that's the price I had to pay, then. Still, I'm not a happy camper. I think one can have both. In fact, I know one can have both, and I berate myself for not being more attentive to my financial responsibilities. I hate myself for this!

I know, I know; I should be grateful for what we have. And I am. But "time's winged chariot is drawing near," and I don't want to leave this world feeling like I did not do right by Penny. I would like us to have a few anxiety-free years before we cross over; but I really don't know if that's going to happen. Penny's job is getting more difficult to do by the day as time catches up to her body, and our savings may run out before we catch up to where we can live anxiety free. If only one of my books would connect. I don't know what to do, Padre. I give up. Do you have any suggestions?

I didn't mean to dump on you like this. Or did I? I had to get it out of my system, and who better to dump on than someone who's heard all of man's worries? Padre, how come you don't visit me in my dreams? Is that asking too much?

Or maybe you do and I just don't remember. That's possible. But what difference would that make? It would only be exciting material for me to write about. I'm a real whore to my Muse, aren't I? God, is there no end to my vanity? I have to stop.

Ciao for now,
Orest

11. *Between Here and Now*

Saturday, April 13, 2013

Dear Padre,

That situation with our tenant seems to be resolving itself. I'll keep you posted. Today I want to talk to you about this feeling of floundering. I'm not floundering, really; it just feels like I am. It's more like a feeling of being between *here* and *there*, only I don't know where *there* is and *here* is starting to wear heavily upon me.

I stopped writing my letter for a few minutes to do a spiritual contemplation on this feeling of being between *here* and *there*, and I got the insight that *there* is a new commitment to creative writing. I say this because of the spiritual musing that I brought to closure yesterday—"The Mystical Power of Story."

This musing revealed to me that story is the **secret way of life**, and I have a feeling welling up inside of me of going back to literature—poetry, short stories, and novels—to consolidate my talent as a creative writer.

I can't help but feel that I am going to be reading a lot of literature, exploring the short story genre by reading short stories to inspire me to start writing short stories, which I've been putting off for far too long now. And I'm going to get back into reading poetry again, because poetry exercises my creative muscles like no other genre. And I may even write a poem or two when the spirit moves me, just to solidify myself.

Actually, Padre; I've been feeling sorry for myself lately. That's why the *here* of my life is starting to weigh heavily upon me. I think about all the things that I have to do—personal responsibilities, and whatnot—and fear grips me and I recoil into denial.

This is not a good place to be; so by fanning the flame of my literary interests I may just lift myself about this debilitating state of consciousness. What do you think?

To tell you the truth, I could use a little feng shui in my life now; and by this I mean that I should unclutter my life so the Chi can flow freely. Get my writing room cleaned up. I've got books everywhere. My desk is loaded with books that I have been using for my writing, and there are books scattered on the floor. It's a writer's hovel!

It's only logical, isn't it? If I want more inspiration in my life, I have to unclutter my life so the Chi (the vital life force) can flow more freely in my life. The truth is, I know what to do; but I don't have the **doing energy**. I need more **doing energy.** This brings to mind a saying that I came across when I was into long distance running: a body at rest stays at rest, and a body in motion stays in motion. Which translates into this: to get **doing energy** I have to **do**; and the trick is to just get started, because I know from experience that once I get started I create **doing momentum,** and this will transport me from *here* to *there*!

I have a list of what I would like to **do** when I get *there*: 1. I would like to excite my life by improving my health—like doing regular exercise. 2. I would like to read at least one poem and/or short story every day, if at all possible. 3. I would like to attend to my household responsibilities this summer—painting the house, and whatnot. I want to do this for Penny. She's been far too patient with me. And I want to do my spiritual contemplations on a regular basis; meaning, at least once a day. All of this, of course, aside from my daily writing—which keeps me sane in the *here* of my life!

So, Padre; what do you say? Give me a boot to get me started. I could use a good kick in the butt! That's all for now,

Until the next time,
Your procrastinating companion,
Orest

12. *Writing for Posterity*

Dear Padre,

It's not a thought that I want to contemplate, but it's beginning to creep up on me with each passing day—I think that I'm writing for posterity!

At first, this thought terrified me; because it suggested that I would never get to see the fruits of many years of writing. But now I feel a sense of relief, because I don't have the pressure of not "making it" in the marketplace; and I don't mind that now, really.

It's enough to know that I have published some of my best work, so it is on record; but just because none of my work has connected with the reading public yet doesn't meant that it won't someday. Sometimes it takes a long time for a book to connect. I just wish that I could see it in my lifetime. But now I have the feeling that I'm writing for posterity.

And that's okay. As long as I keep writing. In fact, I have the quiet conviction that I have a few more books to get out before I shuffle off this mortal coil. I'm not quite there yet, but I do feel that I won't leave this world until I get these other books out. Which books these are, I'm not quite sure. It could be the one I just finished, *The Summoning of Noman, Cathedral of My Past Lives, St. Paul's Conceit, The Waking Dream,* and

The Seeker, Quest for the Lost Soul of God; plus my next book with you—which I believe I'm going to call *Padre Pio Speaks from Heaven.*

I honestly don't know what's going on. I just keep plugging along, hoping for the best. As you said, *"Live, love, and enjoy your life; and don't worry about tomorrow. Tomorrow never comes. There is only today."* That's a great way to look at life. I wish I could live this way every day. All I can do is try.

Penny made a wonderful dinner last night. She made cabbage rolls and I brought home perogies and low fat sour cream from the store. And she baked a raisin pie. We had our neighbors over for dinner and a friend who came up to her cottage for the weekend. Our neighbors brought their famous Caesar salad.

I put on a little fire in our Pacific wood stove, and our sun room and kitchen had that warm, comfortable feeling that put us all at ease; and we had a lovely dinner and conversation. Our guests did not want to leave. And of course Penny had to give our guests some cabbage rolls to take home. Our friend said to Penny, "No-one ever goes hungry in your house." Which made Penny feel really good.

Penny and I know that the energy is our house is a healing energy; that's why our guests love coming to dinner. It's a healing experience for them. I'd sure like to know how this healing energy works its way into their life. Perhaps you can give me a hint, by way of a dream or something. It would satisfy my curiosity.

In any event Padre, I just wanted to touch base. I was working on a spiritual musing ("10,000 Hours, Past Lives, or Luck of the Draw"), which I just finished, so I put off writing you; but I'm free now, until my next musing that is.

I'm doing the final edit of my first book of letters to you so Penny can get it published. She created the cover already, and it's beautiful. It has a butterfly motif; two cupped hands releasing butterflies. The picture is called "concept of freedom." We hope to have the first volume of my letters to you published next month, and I can't wait to see what kind of response we're going to get.

So, what do you think Padre; am I writing for posterity?

Ciao for now,
Your faithful companion,
Orest

13. *A Dangerous Time of Year*

Sunday, April 28, 2013

Dear Padre,

I'm just getting over a head cold. It began with the sniffles last week and my head began to get stuffed up, but as Penny's father likes to say, it did not "grab me." By that I mean it didn't move into my chest entirely, only partially; but had it grabbed me I would have probably had to go to the doctor for antibiotics. Instead I dosed up on vitamin C and Echinacea (tablets as well as tea), and managed to keep it from settling into my chest. And with Penny's advice, I put Vic's Vaporizing Cold Rub on my chest every night before bed. This helped me sleep because it warded off the coughing.

I had to finish a small drywall taping job in Wasaga for a contractor, and it was not pleasant working with this cold. It was very fatiguing. I only worked two and three hour days, but I did finish it; and was I glad because I could concentrate on just resting. That's the best cure for colds—a lot of rest, which I enjoyed with relish.

I'm still sniffling a little, so I can't take any chances. This is what I call "a dangerous time of year," because the sun is getting warmer but the air is still cold, and one puts his defenses down and doesn't dress properly and the cold air penetrates the body taxing the immune system and leaving one vulnerable to the nasty viruses in the air; so I've been staying indoors, except for yesterday. I went into Midland for my weekend paper and the May 2013 *Harper's* and *New Yorker* magazines, and I also picked up some fresh fruit and veggies for our nutri-blast smoothies.

I did have some coughing spells that brought back memories of when I had to be hospitalized for bronchitis just before I was diagnosed with a heart condition which led to my bypass operation, and I became acutely conscious again of my own mortality, and I had some serious moments of reflection; but I don't want to dwell on that now. Suffice to say that I know my clock is running out of time, and I have miles to go and promises to keep before I drop this mortal coil...

On another note, Penny sent out my manuscript of *The Summoning of Noman* yesterday to Hay House Insights Nonfiction Writing Contest. First prize is a five thousand dollar advance and a publishing package with Balboa Press. Wouldn't it be nice? This would give me the exposure my writing needs. I can only hope.

I've been doing a lot of thinking lately about this new state of consciousness that I seem to have quietly moved into, a state of asexual consciousness that sets me apart from the rest of the world. Last night I was watching a movie (I think it was called *A Perfect Ending*), about a woman and mother of three children whose relationship with her husband had lost its intimacy. She's dying of cancer, and she has a sexual relationship with a younger woman that opens her up to a love she never knew she was capable of; and as I watched the sexual love scenes with these two women I had to smile because I felt like an alien from another planet peeking into the "strange" behavior of those two women.

There was a time (and not that long ago) when I would have been sexually aroused by those love scenes, but not last night. The strange thing about this new state of asexual consciousness is that I feel like I'm in the world but not of the world. It's an amazing place to be, and I honestly think this is what you meant by a state of karma-free consciousness that we talked about in my spiritual healing sessions. And this state of asexual consciousness that I'm in now goes a long way to explaining what you meant when you said, "Karma is a choice." I honestly think I understand that now.

From this completely non-attached state of asexual consciousness I knew that I had a choice to dive in, as it were, into the sexual state of consciousness—if I wanted to experience sexual arousal; but I chose not to. And speaking of choice, this also happened in a dream a few nights ago. I could have chosen to dive into a sexual experience in my dream, but I chose not to—thereby avoiding the karma of the experience.

This opens up to the question of experiencing life without incurring karma. I experienced life last night as

I watched the movie. I deliberately allowed myself to pay close attention to the sexual scenes—which were pretty intense, though decorous—but I was not pulled into that state of sexual consciousness that normally would have engaged me within seconds before I gravitated to this new state of detached consciousness. So what's going on here, Padre? Have I transcended myself?

You did tell me that I had transcended my own voice and the voice of my spiritual community, but this seems to be something new entirely. I can gauge my new state of self-transcendence every time I watch TV. I never realized how much a role sex plays in life. It's like the air we breathe. It's everywhere, and I feel like I'm breathing it like everyone else but I'm not affected by it like everyone else. Is this what Jesus meant by being in the world but not of the world? Is this what it means to be centered in one's Soul self, which is above the sensual planes of material consciousness?

I don't know, Padre; but something is happening to me, and I like it. I have never felt so free inside as I do now. And this is only the start of it. I can feel new horizons of spiritual freedom just waiting for me to enter into. But I can't precipitate them. I know they will come when I'm ready, and only then; but I can feel them coming.

I just had another thought. Is this new spiritual freedom coming to me because of my new spiritual musings? Is there a relationship with the freedom-energy (the spiritual consciousness of my new musings) that readers of my spiritual musings blog are picking up and which is being returned to me in spades (because this is how karma works: we get back what we put out) thereby precipitating my own transcendence?

I know definitely that there is a very mysterious relationship between writer and reader. This relationship is so mystical that I don't even want to touch upon it now for the fear of learning what I suspect is very dangerous knowledge, and by this I mean knowledge that would frighten one from putting his thoughts into books. I've hinted at this before, which is why I said that I would not want to be in Stephen King's shoes, nor Anne Rice's. These writers scare me with what they have put out there.

What they have put out there in their writing doesn't scare me; how what they put out there affects their personal state of consciousness (their karmic body, if you will) scares me; because it seems to me that the more you enmesh a soul with the thoughts and images that you put out there, the more enmeshed you become—which goes against one's predestined spiritual purpose in life, which is spiritual liberation from the consciousness of these lower worlds. This is why Jesus said, *"Straight is the gate and narrow is the way, which leadeth unto life, and few there be that find it"* (Math. 7: 14).

And this opens up a whole new thought that I've been entertaining lately—the thought of the coexistence of parallel worlds—each world affecting the other in the omnipresent NOW. This is too big for me to wrap my mind around, so I'm going to leave that for now. I want to grow into this thought a little more before I explore it. That's all for today, Padre...

I remain,
Your grateful spiritual companion,
Orest

14. *My New Hilroy Notebooks*

Dear Padre,

I seem to be getting over my cold. I thought for a while that it was going to morph into bronchitis, but it seems to be going away. I'm not coughing as much. I think it was the large doses of Vitamin C that I've been taking, in tablets and citrus juice; or you may have intervened when I talked to you on my drive home from Midland.

I was really under the weather yesterday morning when I drove into Midland to pick up my Saturday paper (*The National Post*), and on my drive home I thought about the reading and talk on the creative process and spirituality that I was planning to do at a friend's house at the end of the month. Every spring she organizes a little group of people to show their artwork and she invited me again, and I said to you, "I won't be going if this cold hangs on. So if you want me to go, do something about it please; otherwise I won't go. One way or the other, it doesn't matter to me. It's in Spirit's hands..."

Those may not be the exact words, but the point I was making was that if it was meant for me to go, then I'd be cured of my lingering cold; and to be quite honest with you Padre, my coughing was starting to scare me. I've been down with bronchitis before, and those coughing bouts can be frightening. Anyway, I came home from Midland and lay down for a few hours and actually slept; and when I got up I was so thirsty that I drank three glasses of citrus juice that I had picked up in Midland, and believe it or not I think I'm on the mend. I've been drinking more citrus juice, and I plan to go into Midland and pick up some more today when I go for my Sunday paper (*The Toronto Star*).

I also picked up two Hilroy notebooks because I plan to start a new regimen for writing: in one notebook I plan to record all the new words and descriptive phrases that I come across in my reading (I plan to immerse myself in short story reading to prepare myself for short story writing), and in my second notebook I plan to record all the memorable quotations from every book that I read. I want to have a record of those quotations that speak to me in that special way that announce the Way.

I think you know what I mean by this. For example, in the book *The Fiery Muse, Creativity and the Spiritual Quest*, by Teri Degler, she wrote a lot of things that spoke to me—like this: **"one of the primary elements in the internal battle most of us go through in our creative work: we struggle to learn not to struggle"** (p. 3).

I want to keep a record of these memorable quotes because they may help me in my own journey through life, and they will come in handy for my writing when I need to express a particular thought. So

51

by recording new words and descriptive phrases I will add to my writing vocabulary, and recording new quotes will add to my gnostic wisdom of life, and this will add new depth and texture to my writing; or so I hope.

Actually, the reason I want to initiate this new literary regimen is because I am being strongly pulled to story writing. I don't know why, but it seems that I have come to that point in my writing where I have to dive into the simple mystery of life itself through the story—like the idea for my story "Regression."

I ran this idea by Penny yesterday as we sat on our front deck and she liked it very much. It's the story of a young lady who studies psychology at university. It was my wish to study psychology, become a Jungian analyst, and then combine this Jungian therapy with past-life regressions; but since I'm much too old to do this, I can create a character in my story to become a Jungian therapist who incorporates past-life regressions into her practice; hence, my title "Regression." Because it would center upon one of her patients who finds out why he is gender-conflicted when he is regressed to seven consecutive female past lives. Reincarnation explores the reason for gender confliction.

This would be the theme of my story. I don't know if it would be a novella, or a novel; but I'd really like to explore this theme. But before I get to this story I would like to write a few short stories first; so I'm getting ready for my adventure into story writing by immersing myself in short story reading just to get the flavor of the short story from some of the world's best short story writers—like Alice Munroe, Mavis Gallant, John Updike, and of course the *New Yorker* magazine short stories that are published monthly just so I can stay abreast of contemporary short story writing.

What do you think, Padre? Am I on the right track? In one of my spiritual healing sessions the lady who channeled you told me after you said that I should be writing more from the heart that she saw a pen, paper, and a heart—indicating that I would be writing from the heart. So, is that where I'm headed?

That's all for today...

I am,

Your faithful companion,

Orest

15. *My Forgotten Novel*

Tuesday, May 7, 2013

Dear Padre,

Funny, how things work out; I picked up a novel that I wrote thirteen years ago in my hometown. It was in a grey binder sitting on a pile of blue binders and papers in a cardboard box in the corner of my writing room. I was in my reading chair and the grey binder caught my attention, so I picked it up and started reading.

I had forgotten that I had written this novel, but it engaged me from the first few lines and I kept on reading. It's called *Grace,* and it's the story of my Platonic relationship with an ex nun from Newfoundland whose house I painted.

Padre, I couldn't help but feel that you were looking over my shoulder as I read through my forgotten novel; and I got the strongest urge to work on it and get it published, which I think I am going to do. But unfortunately I don't have it on my hard drive, nor do I have it saved on my old floppy discs or data traveler; so I may have to retype the whole manuscript. But that's okay, because typing the manuscript will get me back into the feel of the story. So what do you say, should I go ahead with it?

The novel is 245 pages single spaced in manuscript form, so it will take me about two weeks to retype, if not more; but by the time I get it done I should be very much into the atmosphere of my story and will know where to improve upon it.

Several weeks to retype, and three or four weeks to edit and proof and it should be ready; but I won't be free to work on it as I would like, because this summer Penny wants me to paint the house and clean up a few other household responsibilities. But I want to go ahead with the project. I may even start today.

This novel reveals the conflict that I had with my Roman Catholic faith, and the dialogue that I have with Grace Kendal sheds a great deal of light on why I left the Church at such a young age. But it's more of Grace's story than mine.

I think I have your nod on this one, Padre; so I probably will start working on it today. I'll keep you posted...

Your faithful companion,
Orest

16. *The Haircut that Shocked My Psyche*

Wednesday, May 15, 2013

Dear Padre,

I remember when I used to have a barber cut my hair, but now it's a hair stylist, and quite often a woman; and I have always had trouble getting a nice haircut. So I changed barbers often when I lived up north. But ever since we moved to Georgian Bay I found a hair stylist who gave me such a wonderful cut that I kept going to her regularly, until she quit her job last year; and I had to try someone else, but not to my satisfaction.

That was three haircuts ago, and all three preyed upon my mind because they did not leave me with a good feeling. I simply did not find them satisfactory, especially today's haircut which shocked my psyche. So, Padre; I'm not in the best of moods.

In fact, as I write you this letter I am wearing one of the three baseball caps that a friend and neighbor gave me for Christmas last year; that's how I feel about the haircut I got this morning. And when Penny called from work at lunch I told her about my haircut and asked her not to laugh at me when she comes home. She can laugh behind my back, but not in front of me; that's how uncomfortable I feel about my haircut.

Now you may well ask, is that vanity? Of course it's vanity! What the hell else can it be? I just did not expect my psyche to be shocked by the way I looked when my hair stylist (or is it hairdresser?) was done with my hair.

Here's what happened. I always let my hair grow long. My hair is curly, so I let it grow long because I like it when my hair curls up. And I often grow it at least one or two months longer than I should before I get a haircut; but I prefer it longer than shorter. But guess what happened today? I got the shortest haircut of my life—*a buzz cut!*

All my curls are gone, and now you can see that my hair on the front of my head is thinning out and the pink scalp is showing through, which is not noticeable when my hair is long. Like Samson, I feel I lost my strength. That's why I'm wearing a ball cap. Vain, or what?

Who cares? I'm really pissed at myself. I told my hair stylist to use the electric clippers, just like my old stylist used to do. She used the electric clippers to trim down my hair to a certain length, and then she styled it with her scissors; but I had forgotten the number that she used for the clippers.

Let me explain: They have an attachment that goes onto the electric clippers that cuts the hair to a certain length. There are eight attachments. I couldn't remember what number my old stylist used, so I asked my new stylist to use number five. This was a big mistake, because once she started (after washing my hair) she had to continue, but the clippers cut my hair so short that she had very little left to style with her scissors.

I tried to put on a brave face, but I was boiling inside for my stupidity. I should have asked her to start with the longest and work my way down; but I started with a number that cut my hair so short that when she was finished it shocked my psyche. And good God, do I feel like a bloody fool for being so impetuous. Why couldn't I inquire first instead of giving her the go-ahead without knowing what length my hair was going to be?

I'm so angry at myself that I told Penny on the phone that I am not going to go to our friends' home in southern Ontario next weekend for their arts potluck lunch and arts gathering. I was going to read from my first volume of *Letters to Padre Pio* (the essay that I included in the addendum called "A Timeless Wisdom,") and I was going to give a talk on the creative process; but my bloody vanity won't allow me to go now!

I should mention also that I still haven't got a plate for the tooth that I lost last year; and that doesn't help boost my confidence. So I am depriving myself of a wonderful opportunity to be with friends and other artists just because I have not been on top of my life; so what did I do when I got home?

I sulked for an hour, and then I dug up "The Eye of Revelation," by Peter Kelder. This is a photocopied manuscript that a fellow heart patient gave me when we were doing post-surgery cardiac workouts at the Collingwood hospital three years ago. The subtitle is: "The Original Five Tibetan Rites of Rejuvenation." And I'm going to incorporate these five rites of rejuvenation into my program—which I haven't started yet, but which that shock to my psyche has motivated me to start because I'm so bloody tired of being one half, if not one third the man I used to be.

I have to get my physical self-confidence back, Padre. I lost it with my by-pass operation, and I have been dragging my ass ever since. But when I saw myself in the hairdresser's mirror I was horrified, as though my age hit me in one devastating blow; and if I don't get off my ass this time and do something to get my body in shape—which means losing some weight!—I may just never get another opportunity. I had to vent, Padre. I hope you can bear with me. That's all for now.

Until again,
Your faithful companion,
Orest

17. *The Meaning of One's Life*

Dear Padre,

I just drove Penny to the Go Bus depot in Barrie. She's going to Toronto to catch a flight to Thunder Bay to be with her father who is in critical condition and not expected to last much longer. Penny's two sisters are with him and her brother is flying in from out west also, so Mel's family will be by his side when he crosses over; so, Padre, if you don't mind, would you please be there with Penny's father for his last days.

I know it's not something one should admit to, but I couldn't help myself this morning as I drove Penny to Barrie. I said to her, "I envy your father, on the verge of crossing over. It's a nice place to be."

I thought this might upset Penny, but it didn't. On the contrary, she agreed with me, telling me that many times she's gone to sleep hoping that she would cross over; that's how tired she was of life also. So we're of like mind.

But what does this say about us? We're certainly not suicidal. The truth is very simple: we suffer from life-fatigue. We're old souls, and we've been around this block so many times that we're tired of the same old same old, and we want out. This opens the door to a very interesting subject: the meaning of one's life.

I've come to some pretty solid conclusions about the meaning of one's life; my life in particular. I can't speak for anyone else's life, but I can extrapolate from the meaning of my life. Being human, I'm like everyone else—you know, the old Socratic syllogism: all men are mortal, Socrates is a man; ergo Socrates is mortal. In like manner, once I determine the meaning of my life I can logically discern the meaning of everyone's life. So, just what is the meaning of my life?

Broadly speaking, I know that I came into this world to find my way out of this world; and the only way I could find my way out was to break the cycle of life and death—i. e., the cycle of karma and reincarnation. To do this I had to find the exit door, which Jesus called the "narrow way."

"Strait is the gate and narrow is the way and few there be that find it," said Jesus, and I found it. Thanks to Gurdjieff's teaching of "work on oneself" I awakened to the Word, which I "heard" in the sayings of Jesus, and after years of living the Word, which is the Way (the "narrow way" to be exact) I shifted my center of gravity from my lower self to my higher self (what Jesus called rebirth) and broke the cycle of karma and reincarnation. And in doing so I satisfied my longing to find my true self, which was my motivation for becoming a spiritual seeker.

This was the implicit purpose of my life—to find my true self. And because I found my true self I have a perspective on life now that few people have; and from this perspective I can safely say that this is the implicit purpose of everyone's life—to find one's true self. This is why Padre you told me in one of my spiritual healing sessions that "life is a journey of the self." We are all on this journey to our true self; and our true self is Soul.

In effect, the meaning of one's life then is to grow in consciousness until we become aware of our divine nature which lies dormant in all of us. But since Nature cannot do this for us, because Nature is governed by the laws of karma and reincarnation and therefore keeps us trapped within the paradigm of life and death, we have to take matters into our own hands and shift ourselves out of nature's closed paradigm. As the ancient Gnostics used to say, we have to complete what nature left unfinished.

But it gets tricky here, Padre; because not everyone has evolved enough to become conscious seekers of the Way. Most people are driven by their unconscious need to be their true self. This is why people are driven the way they are in whatever direction their personal karma compels them to go— meaning, we all have our own karmic destiny; and only by satisfying our karmic destiny can we realize our true self.

My karmic destiny was to find the Way. I came into this world with the specific purpose of finding the Way. I was driven to become a writer, and through the process of satisfying my need to become a writer I was introduced to the secret path of the creative process which awakened me to the Way.

But that was my way to find the Way. I found it through the creative process, but another person may find it through his work as a medical doctor, another through their work teaching school, and another through music—like Victor L. Wooten did, for example, which he recorded in his inspiring novel *The Music Lesson, A Spiritual Search for Growth Through Music;* and another through art, like Jerry Wennstrom who recorded his journey in his magnificent book *The Inspired Heart.*

In a word, the Way is an individual path; and we all come into this world to satisfy our karmic purpose. And as we satisfy our karmic purpose—which simply means that we have to honor our soul's contract with life—we give our life meaning. It's when we fight our own karmic purpose that we fall into the insidious trap of meaninglessness and the many ills that it engenders—like dread, anxiety, and existential despair.

Of course, the question arises: how do we know that we are on the right course in life? How do we know that we are living our karmic purpose? And this is where all the confusion arises, because no-one can tell us for sure. This is something that we have to figure out for ourselves. This is why life is so complicated.

I couldn't figure it out and I suffered like hell. Some people figure it out very early in life. They know exactly what they want to do with their life. Like the girl who knows that she wants to be a nurse; the boy who knows that he wants to be a landscape architect; and the girl who knows that she wants to be a singer.

When a person knows what they want to do form the earliest age and do everything in their power to become what they want to be, they are fulfilling their karmic purpose in life.

But as I said, we don't all know what we want to do; which makes our life very complicated because we don't have a definite karmic purpose to guide us. We have to play it by ear as it were, until we hit upon the right course that will satisfy our inner longing to be our true self. It's all one big puzzle, isn't it Padre?

Which reminds me of something you said in another spiritual session. You likened life unto a joke, and we wouldn't get the punch line until we got to the Other Side. Well, I get the joke, Padre. I get it so much that I don't have to wait to get to the Other Side. This is why I said to Penny that I did not envy her father's position. Unlike him, though (who is hanging on for dear life), I am ready to cross over.

Believe you me, when my time comes I will not be fighting my entry to the Other Side; but only when I have fulfilled my karmic obligations to this life. And I know that won't be until I satisfy my longing to write the books that I still have inside me!

That's all for today, Padre...

Ciao for now,
Your faithful companion,
Orest

18. *A Bee in My Window*

Friday, June 14, 2013

Dear Padre,

I want to share a curious but exciting little coincidence with you. It just happened a few minutes ago. I was typing my "forgotten novel" (*Tea with Grace, A Story of Platonic Love* which I wrote thirteen years ago) into my word processor, Chapter 8 ("A Soul Moment"), when I heard a bee buzzing in my window.

I turned to look and saw that it was flying about in between my partially opened window and the screen; it was trying to fly through the glass to escape.

It couldn't escape, because it kept flying into the glass. It didn't know enough to fly back out through the crack of the opened window, so it kept buzzing as it tried to fly through the clear glass.

I got up and opened the window wide, giving the bee a much larger crack between the window and screen; and within a few seconds it found the larger crack and flew away and I went back to typing my manuscript; and here's when I experienced the exciting meaningful little coincidence, which I have to call synchronistic.

I was typing that part of my story when Grace (a married ex nun) asks Oriano (her spiritually eclectic house painter and writer) what he meant by telling her that he had outgrown his Christian faith. Grace is in a quandary, because she can't see that life has brought her to the limits of her Roman Catholic faith, and she has no room to grow within the strict confines of her faith; and Oriano has been trying to get her to see that if she wants to satisfy her soul's irrepressible need for spiritual growth she has to expand her faith. But she has no idea what that means, and she's puzzled.

That's when the bee flew into the narrow space between the glass of my window and the screen, and the buzzing was interrupting my concentration; so I stopped typing and went to the window to help the bee escape from the confines of the window-screen space.

I rolled the handle of my window opener and widened the crack between the window and screen. The bee buzzed around bumping into the clear glass and I cracked the window open wider and finally the bee flew out into the open space of the great outdoors. The bee symbolizes Grace trapped by her rigid Roman Catholic faith, and my opening the window for the bee to escape symbolizes Oriano's efforts to expand Grace's faith (opening of the window of her soul, as it were) so she can escape.

But does she escape?

I hate to be a spoiler, but sadly she does not escape. Grace has too much invested in her faith to take the next step in her journey to the Far Country of God. But all the same, I think *Tea with Grace* is a wonderful story that addresses a lot of issues that

Christians will have to face some day; and to think that I had forgotten I had written this novel!

Thanks for nudging me to pick up my old manuscript, Padre. Believe it or not, I think this is the best thing that I have ever written!

Ciao for now,
Your faithful companion,
Orest

19. *Blessing or Disappointment*

Monday, June 24, 2013

Dear Padre,

I had a strange experience yesterday that I'm still trying to work out. It had to do with a friend's friend whom I was looking forward to meeting. I was told by my friend that her octogenarian friend was a Jungian therapist, and I wanted to meet her just for the experience of meeting a student of Jung's psychology; but this proved to be a non-starter.

I sent my friend's friend an email with an attached letter, which I titled "By Way of Introduction," but she received my attached file with the warning: "Letters to F may contain an application. The safety of this file cannot be determined." Wisely, she did not open my file; so she never got to read my letter.

This was either a blessing or a disappointment; I haven't decided which yet. But I'm leaning towards a blessing, because I suspect by the comments in her reply email that I was ***"too much information"*** for her. I use the phrase "too much information" on purpose, because this is what the omniscient guiding force of life, highlighted for me while I was reading the newspaper yesterday morning on the deck when I shared my thoughts with Penny on the comments that F made in her reply to me, about her desire to keep my emails simple, that she did not want "a whole bunch of stuff to read."

Just as I shared with Penny that she did not want "a whole bunch of stuff to read" the line I was reading in the paper *("too much information")* jumped out at me, and I knew by the synchronistic pairing of these two things that Spirit was telling me that I was too much for my friend's friend, and that our relationship was a non-starter.

This saddened me at first because I was looking forward to talking with a student of Jung's psychology, but the more I thought about it the more I came to terms with how it came to be a non-starter: I realized that the omniscient guiding force of life did not want me to have a relationship with my friend's friend.

Why, I don't know just yet; but I have a feeling that my energy would have been too much for her to handle, and it would have disturbed the tonality of her frequency. So Spirit gave me an opportunity to not pursue it, which is what I'm going to do.

With my blessings then, I'm going to say to my friend's friend: "Thank you, but no thank you. May the gods of destiny be kind to you."

In all honesty, I really would have liked to meet a Jungian student because I have so much respect for C. G. Jung and his contribution to world thought. So if I may, could you possibly arrange for me to meet a genuine Jungian student, someone who has the same appreciation for Jung's work as I do; because I'd love nothing more than to discuss my understanding of

Jung's insights with someone with an equal love for them?

You know what, Padre? I'd like to share the letter I wrote to my friend's friend, just so we can have it on record; so, if you will indulge me:

Letter to F
By Way of Introduction
Sunday, June 23, 2013

Hi F,

If I may take the liberty, I'd like to tell you why I'd like to meet up with you and talk about C. G. Jung. J told me a while back that she had a Jungian friend, and being an ardent student of Jung's psychology I hoped that one day I would get to meet you because I have yet to meet another student of C. G. Jung. I discovered Jung when I was studying Gurdjieff, whom I "chanced" upon while studying philosophy at university and whose teaching transformed my life; but, ironically, in all the years that I studied Gurdjieff I never met another student of his teaching. I met Gurdjieff in my dreams, and Dr. Maurice Nicoll, who studied with Jung in Switzerland but left Jung to study Gurdjieff's teaching with P. D. Ouspensky, and I have regretted not meeting another student of the Work (G's teaching); and I do not want to repeat my experience. This is why I would like to meet up with you, because I would love the experience of dialoguing with someone whose life has been influenced by the redoubtable C. J. Jung.

As you may know, if you have perused my web page and/or my spiritual musings blog, I am a writer; and, as you may very well suspect, writers always have a private agenda—despite themselves. We write about life, and life is where we find it; and I find in you a golden opportunity to enhance my knowledge of the Jungian perspective on life. I say this because I have already written a novel with Jung as one of my central characters, but this novel is not published yet because I had a lot more research to do on Jung to do him justice, and you can consider my talk with you part of my research; and I also have another novel pressing to be written. This one will feature a young prescient female Jungian therapist as the central character, but with a twist: she is also a past-life regression therapist. That's all I can say about this novel now because I never talk about a book until I have written it. Hemingway taught me this. He said that to talk about a work before writing it is like taking the dust off a butterfly's wings; it loses its magic. Having said this, I do hope that you do not find my objective too forward; but I wanted to be up front with you.

Which leads me to request that we have our first meet-up in private. I know that J would love to sit in on our talk, but I anticipate a dialectical discourse; and this precludes a third party. The dynamics of a dialectic would be disturbed with a third party, meaning no disrespect to J; and I would love to experience the natural, spontaneous flow of our discourse. Which brings to mind Jung's first encounter with Sigmund Freud when they talked non-stop for thirteen hours; but, regrettably, we do not have a record of that conversation, only bits and pieces of it. And this leads me to make an observation, if you will permit me my openness.

I suspect that there are very few people in the world, including Jungians that can truly appreciate C. G. Jung's contribution to world thought. Thank goodness that his family finally allowed his *Red Book* to be published, because it tells the story of the hero's journey into the far country of the soul; and, believe me, the modern world could sure use the mythological import of Jung's amazing quest for his lost soul. *The Red Book* is the hidden, submerged part of the iceberg that all of Jung's writing implies—just like Hemingway's stories. Let me explain:

Hemingway developed a theory for writing his stories. His theory was born of his study of Cézannes art, which he studied for hours in the Louvre when he lived in Paris as a young man. He came to realize that there was a hidden narrative in Cézannes art work, and Hemingway cultivated a way of telling a story by implying the greater part of his story, which he did in his first novel *The Sun Also Rises*. Jake Barnes and Lady Brett Ashley are in love, but they cannot consummate their love sexually because Jake has a war wound that prohibited sexual intercourse; but we, the reader, do not know this. This is all implied in the story, and this gives the story such emotional impact that it launched Hemingway's career as a new and promising young writer.

Ironically, I always sensed Jung's personal narrative in all of his writing; and when I finally got a copy of *The Red Book* last Christmas (I got the Amazon Reader's Edition delivered to my front door here in Georgian Bay on the 28th of December, and I read it through to New Years Day, the most engrossing read of my entire life, making it the best Christmas present I have ever received!) I felt a great sense of relief, because finally I had a conscious understanding of what Jung implied in all of his writing—*his gnostic experience of the Way!*

I shant talk about the Way now, because that's too esoteric at this point; but what made *The Red Book* so fascinating for me was Jung's initiation into the far country of the soul, which very, very few souls ever experience—until they are made ready by life, that is (which, of course, presupposes my belief in reincarnation; but that's another subject). This of course leads me to ask if you have ever practiced "active imagination." But you can tell me this in person.

Being a creative writer, I have experienced "active imagination" many times in my life; with every novel that I write, in fact. And if I may be so bold, my most exciting experience of "active imagination" was writing my novel *Jesus Wears Dockers, The Gospel Conspiracy Story*. I called up an archetypal Jesus and dialogued with him, and the result was an exciting dialectical discourse on the secret meaning of Christ's sayings—a thoroughly enjoyable experience!

This is another reason why I'd love to talk with you, just to share and hear another Jungian's experience and/or knowledge of the exploratory technique of "active imagination." In all honesty, I am convinced that C. J. Jung has not yet come unto his own; and I don't think he will for another twenty-five years or so yet. That's how long I think it will take for the mainstream to catch up to his thinking; which, at the risk of sounding presumptuous, speaks to my writing because I suspect that I am writing for posterity. Which is rather sad, because I would love to experience that mysterious connection with the readers of my books. J, I'm happy to say, has connected with at least one of my books—*Keeper of the Flame*; and I'm very grateful for that.

Have I blathered on enough for you? I just wanted to open the dialogue with some personal information just to fan the flame, as it were; which, if you so desire to respond to, I'd be delighted to receive and ponder and reciprocate.

I look forward to talking with you.

Was that too much information, Padre? I'll never know, will I? I have to take it on trust alone that Divine Spirit was speaking to me when it highlighted the line *"too much information"* just as I was sharing what I did about F's email with Penny. The synchronicity of these two experiences convinced me that Spirit was speaking to me!

I haven't figured out why yet, but I suspect it has to do with the path that one is on in life and how one can disturb the vibrations of one's path. **Unless one is ready for a new frequency, the tonality of one's frequency should not be disturbed.**

I didn't know this, but Divine Spirit did; so it did me a favor and gave me an opportunity to not initiate this relationship. That's all I want to say on the subject for now. Perhaps down the road it will make more sense to me; so, until the next time,

I remain,
Your faithful companion,
Orest

20. *Healing the Wounded Soul*

Sunday, June 30, 2013

Dear Padre,

Penny and I were invited for a barbeque yesterday. Our friends live in a small community north of Orillia. They have a house by the river and we sat on the deck enjoying the afternoon talking and exchanging points of view as the odd pontoon boat motored up and down the river and the odd kayaker silently glided by.

Our friend brought out a bowl of Tostitos and salsa to snack on, and a plate of fresh local strawberries (which are incomparably tastier than the imported strawberries), grapes, and pineapple pieces; and when the time was right I asked my friend who had purchased a copy of *Healing with Padre Pio* from me when she and her husband and another friend visited me a couple of weeks ago (Penny wasn't home; she had to fly up north to be with her father), about her Jungian friend from Orillia that I was looking forward to meeting but changed my mind when I received her email.

"J," I said, probing her because I wanted to satisfy my curiosity about the character of her Jungian friend, whom I had discerned to be "one of Leacock's people" (Stephen Leacock was a Canadian satirist who wrote stories based upon his impressions of people from Orillia where he lived, my favorite book being *Sunset Sketches of a Little Town*), "I got the impression that your Jungian friend is a crusty old broad who's quite fixed in her beliefs. I think she's one of Leacock's people."

J, who was familiar with Leacock's writing, agreed without hesitation, saying that her friend had a wall around her that was not easily penetrated. That's why J wondered how our energies would interact when we met.

But sensing what I did about her octogenarian Jungian friend, I chose not to meet her at all because I had no desire to interact with her crusty energies, which I discerned to be dissonant with mine; but that's not why I'm writing you this letter. I mentioned this simply to bring my thoughts on my friend's Jungian friend to some kind of closure. In short, it wasn't meant for us to meet and now I know why; and I'm writing this letter today because I have something else that I'd like to share with you, an observation that I think you will find interesting, if not delightfully amusing.

The thought for this letter came to me early this morning while I was having coffee on the front deck reading Carolyn Myss's new book *Archetypes*. Whether you planted this thought or not, I don't know (I suspect it was you, but let's just say my Muse planted it), but into my mind popped the phrase "healing the wounded soul," and I *knew* I had to drop what I was doing to catch this thought in a letter to you.

Perhaps something I read in *Archetypes* called up the memory of J's husband's dream of the deer caught in a wire fence that triggered the phrase "healing the wounded soul," but whatever it was I felt instantly compelled to write you a letter to have this insight on record; and my insight has to do with something that you and I talked about in one of my spiritual healing sessions with you.

Do you remember me asking you about the effect that my novel *Healing with Padre Pio* would have upon the readers? I said that because you are the Healing Saint blessed with the miraculous grace of compassionate love (which I believe to be your defining virtue), your energy would affect every reader of *Healing with Padre Pio*; and you agreed. In fact, you replied, "Many, many times." Which meant that many readers of *Healing with Padre Pio* would be touched by the healing grace of your compassionate love.

Well, I'm happy to report that it's started. That's the point of this letter, to confirm that the energy of your compassionate love that imbues *Healing with Padre Pio* has begun to work its magic upon the readers; and I say this because yesterday I witnessed it for the second time at J's house when her husband shared a dream that he had a couple of nights ago, a dream of a deer whose antlers were caught in a wire fence.

In the dream G was driving a school bus (which he does in real life as a part-time job since his retirement, and which he loves because he gets along so well with children), and as he's driving he spots a deer caught in a wire fence. He stops the bus and tells all the children to stay quite.

He very carefully stalks up to the deer, and as he's walking he softly sings the ancient love song to God (the Hu chant, familiar to him from his wife's spiritual path), and with his pair of pliers (which he must have had in the bus) he gently begins to cut the wire that has enmeshed the deer's antlers until the deer is set free and saunters off.

Why, I don't know, but instantly I knew what that dream meant; so I said to G, "Would you like to know what your dream means?"

Of course he said yes, and I told him that the deer was his wounded soul trapped in the wire fence of life; and that his higher self set it free.

Strangely enough (maybe it wasn't so strange) his wife agreed, and she even said that she had recorded her interpretation of the dream in her notebook and went into the house to get it. And here's the point I want to make with this letter: G's dream confirms the healing power of your compassionate love that G's wife connected with when she brought my novel *Healing with Padre Pio* into her house.

J was well into *Healing with Padre Pio* when her husband had his dream, and I made the connection instantly between his dream and your healing energy. And this confirmed another experience I had with Penny's cousin who came up to visit us a few weeks ago because she was in a spiritual quandary which I "know" was precipitated by the compassionate love of your energy from my novel *Healing with Padre Pio* that I gave her when she visited us last summer. Your compassionate love began to heal her wounded soul, which subsequent events proved; but I cannot go into this now because that's a whole other story that I may write about in another letter, a spiritual musing, or quite possible as a short story which I would love to take on.

Maybe I will write it as a short story. The idea excites me. But be that as it may, I just wanted to share with you that I believe you have begun to work your magic with the readers of my novel *Healing with Padre Pio*.

I know it sounds foolish to make this connection, but for me it's not foolish at all because every book is imbued with its own specific consciousness, and *Healing with Padre Pio* is imbued with the consciousness of your compassionate love, which is the energy that one needs to heal their wounded soul.

So, Padre; I have witnessed two examples of how your energy through my novel has begun the miraculous process of healing the wounded soul of those it touches, and I just want to thank you for your gift of love because it gives me great joy to know that *Healing with Padre Pio* is having this effect upon the people it touches. That's all for now.

Your astonished companion,
Orest

21. *The Fog of My Life*

Sunday, July 7, 2013

Dear Padre,

I'm reading a book by transpersonal psychologist Ken Wilber called *Eye to Eye, The Quest for the New Paradigm*, but I confess that after I got half way through "Preface to Third Edition, Revised" I had to skip and start reading chapter one, "Eye to Eye," which I only read partially before skipping to the last chapter called "The Ultimate State of Consciousness," which I thoroughly enjoyed as though all of the preceding chapters were unnecessary for me to read to enjoy his summation and conclusions, and then I went on Amazon to look up his other books, and one in particular called *The Spectrum of Consciousness* which he wrote at the age of twenty-four caught my attention; so I called it up and went on the Amazon Look Inside feature to feel out the brilliant young writer's first book, and the clarity of his thought for one so young made me envious. He reminded me of Colin Wilson who wrote his brilliant book *The Outsider* in his early twenties also.

I've always envied such precocity, and still do to some degree; but I've since come to appreciate that we are all on our own journey through life and we all bring with us our individual talents and karmic destiny. But as I was researching Ken Wilber—(reading portions of his books on the Amazon Look Inside feature) I was forced to reflect upon my unbelievable journey through the fog of my life to get to the simple clarity that I enjoy today—a journey that I would not repeat for the world!

I say this with confidence, Padre. I doubt that you would want to repeat your life of stigmatic suffering. I'm convinced that once was enough for you. In like manner, once through the fog of my life was enough for me. Even the memories of what I had to suffer working my way out of the fog of my life to realize the spiritual clarity that I have today is enough to want me to repress those memories; and if I could I would banish them from my mind never to remember the idiotic decisions of my impetuous, deluded life. But why was I so deluded? That's the question, isn't it Padre?

Or is this simply the natural process of waking up spiritually? Was I destined on this course of spiritually awakening which is why I have such vivid memories now of how I was so lost in the fog of my personal delusions? After all, all of life is an illusion; isn't that what we are told? And we have to wake up to this illusion to be our true self. So by setting myself on this course of finding my true self was I not destined to work my way through the fog of my life? It had to be, because there is no other way to wake up spiritually!

And yet, when I read such precocious writers like Ken Wilber and Colin Wilson (although, I've since checked Colin Wilson out on the Internet and he's still a brilliant man but who seems to be stuck on the mental plane of consciousness, and for all of his knowledge and brilliance I find him rather boring today); but not Ken Wilber. There's something "other" about his brilliance; and I think this "other" is his personal path, which excites my interest because from what I've read so far his fundamental premise of the imminent and transcendental nature of Spirit resonate with my understanding of Spirit (what I have called the *I Am That I Am Principle of life*), and I'm going to order some of his books and explore what he has to say about what he calls "the perennial philosophy" (he borrowed this from Aldous Huxley) and which I know to be the Way. In other words, Padre; I can see that Ken Wilber is an initiate of the Way, and the unique nature of his individuation of the Way in his writing fascinates me. That's why I'd like to read some of his other books.

Having said that, I want to thank you again for the spiritual healing that you gave me, because your grace slew my vanity and pulled me out of that fog of spiritual confusion that I was lost in for so many years; and ever since my healing I've been seeing with so much clarity that I marvel at how I could have been so blind!

I know I have a long way to go yet (the journey never ends, does it?), but at least I no longer feel that I'm living in a fog. I actually feel like I have stepped out of the fog of my life and am experiencing the simple clarity of spiritual awareness. And if this sounds too abstract, let me tell you that ever since I transcended the consciousness of sexuality I no longer get excited by everything sexual that used to so easily excite my libido before my experience of sexual transcendence about six months ago.

This sounds strange, and hard to believe; but it's true. I have transcended that band of vibrations responsible for sexual consciousness that humanity is trapped in. This fog of sexual consciousness is so thick that very few people even know they are trapped by it; they are so much a part of the fog of sexuality that they can't even conceive of what it would mean to be above it, to not be so affected by it. But I can tell you, it's liberating!

You have to experience the freedom that comes with this state on non-sexual consciousness (not asexual consciousness, but non-sexual; there is a difference); from this perspective when I see people trapped in the fog of sexual consciousness it seems like I am looking at a very strange species. And if I didn't know better, I would ask questions like: what are they doing touching their lips like that? Why are they groping and grabbing each other like that? What is this strange behavior?

That's how far removed I feel from the consciousness of sexuality that has fogged up man's mind so badly that it permeates every aspect of social behavior.

I don't know how I got on this topic, Padre; but maybe it's because I was also so trapped by the fog of sexual consciousness that I needed a miracle to liberate myself—a miracle which you provided with my spiritual healing!

And at the risk of stepping out on a limb here, I suspect my new state of transcendent sexual consciousness speaks to what you called living a karma-free life. I honestly think I'm beginning to know what that actually means—*a state of unaffected awareness!*

Enough about that. I wanted to tell you that as much as I was hoping to begin our project for our next book together this summer, it may not happen yet; I have other books that I have to get out, and our house to paint and other duties to tend to. But I do look forward to our next book together. I have a feeling that it will be more than I expected when I first conceived the idea. I feel it will be about a new spirituality...

Ciao for now,
Your faithful companion,
Orest

22. *The Why of When*

Dear Padre,

I've asked myself the last few years, when are my books going to connect with the reader? You told me in one of my spiritual healing sessions that it would take three years for *Healing with Padre Pio* to trickle out and connect with the reader, and I know that we're only on the second year, but I'm impatient; after all, I do have other books published that could connect with the reader—but they're not. And this bothers me.

Well, yesterday I was out on my front deck reading *Sacred Contracts, Awakening Your Divine Potential* by Caroline Myss; and she wrote something that jumped out at me. It was as though my concern was answered by the Golden-tongued Wisdom (the Voice of Holy Spirit) in a foretelling dream that Caroline Myss had.

She was the only passenger in a small but highly powered jet plane waiting to take flight, but she got word from the control tower to turn her motor off. "We're holding you until the skies are safe for your journey," said the control tower; and Caroline woke up from her dream feeling content to wait for her appropriate time of departure. On the next page Caroline shared the following: "In that occupation (she was a secretary for a political and financial organization) I learned one of the most spiritually productive truths that I now rely on each day of my life: *when you do not seek or need external approval, you are at your most powerful. Nobody can disempower you emotionally or psychologically"* (italics mine).

Caroline Myss needed time to prepare for her flight, and by flight her dream was talking about her future profession as a medical intuitive and writer; and when she was ready, she did indeed take flight. She wrote *Anatomy of Spirit* and it launched her career; so, Padre, I got the point that I'm not quite ready yet to take flight. That was the message that Divine Spirit gave me yesterday; and, in all honesty, I feel that all of this reading and research that I have been doing ever since I wrote *Healing with Padre Pio* is making me ready for my flight—which I sense is going to be next summer!

Believe it or not, I no longer seek or need external approval for my writing, which was one of my most desperate longings; and when I'm totally confident in my spiritual perspective on life I know that my plane will be launched. It's going to take one more year of reading and research to consolidate my perspective, and then "the skies will be safe" for my journey into my writing career.

I don't know this for certain, but I'm reasonably confident; because when I look back at what I've been doing ever since I published *Healing with Padre Pio* I can see that it's all been preparation to make the sky safe for my journey. And by this I mean that the omniscient guiding force of life knows what's awaiting me when I take flight, and I have to be prepared to meet the public with my spiritual perspective. This is why you told me that I will (and you stressed the word WILL) rely upon my own beliefs, which you said will serve me in good stead when I have to defend the ground of my spiritual perspective.

I'm enjoying the book *Sacred Contracts*. It has helped to clarify my mission in life, which I always felt would sound much too presumptuous if I spelled it out; but when I see my mission in terms of a "sacred contract", it makes it much easier to acknowledge that I came into the world to bring some clarity to life's purpose. That's why I look forward to our next book together. Hopefully, we can start next spring.

That's all for now...

As always,
Your trusting companion,
Orest

23. *In My Element*

Dear Padre,

Penny came home from work and I was in the kitchen preparing dinner (I had a stir fry going, rice boiling and chicken in the oven) and she told me she had picked up the mail on her way home and my books were in. She handed me the notice for my parcel and said, "You can pick them up at Jug City tomorrow."

"I'll go right now," I said, all excited. "Keep an eye on dinner for me, please," and I took the parcel notice and drove to Jug City and picked up the box containing the twelve books that Penny had ordered from my Amazon wish list for my birthday.

Jug City was only a few minutes away, so I was back in no time; and when I came into the house I put the box on the kitchen table and opened it and took out the books slowly, one by one. Penny was smiling, enjoying the pleasure that her birthday gift was giving me; and when I had all the books on the table I said, "I can't wait to sit on the deck and check them out."

Which I did, and all evening long I was in my element. I even put the deck lights on so I could stay longer, despite the pesky mosquitoes. I went through each book reading introductions, prologues, and one chapter here, another chapter there; and I settled on starting with *Frequency* first, by the intuitive empath Penny Peirce. But here's the list of books that Penny ordered from my Amazon wish list:

Frequency, The Power of Personal Vibration, by Penney Peirce
Conscious Dreaming, by Robert Moss
The Secret History of Dreaming, by Robert Moss
The Spectrum of Consciousness, by Ken Wilber
Grace and Grit, by Ken Wilber
Ego and Archetype, by Edward F. Edinger
The Gnostic Jung, by Robert A. Segal
C. G. Jung and the Humanities, by Susan Rowland
Evolutionary Enlightenment, by Andrew Cohen
Synchronicity, by Dr. Kirby Surprise
The Power of Coincidence, by David Rico
The Power of Flow, by Charlene Belitz and Meg Lundstrom

So, Padre; it looks like I'm going to have my nose in a book for a while, and I can't wait to get them all read so I can order the other books on my wish list because I need them all to ready myself so my "jet plane" can take flight.

I need these books to be informed about cutting edge thought, especially Penney Peirce's book *Frequency* (I have to order the other two books of her trilogy, *The Intuitive Way,* and *Leap of Perception*), because she's on the edge of the cutting edge—which is where I believe my writing is; that's why I have to be informed for when one of my books connects and I have to go into the arena of life and speak about my books.

Now, if I'm not mistaken in one of my spiritual healing sessions you held up a book for "Angie" (who channeled you) to see, and I have the strongest suspicion that that book was *Frequency*, by Penney Peirce; right?

I think it was, because this book addresses my perception about personal vibrations and the new spirituality; but I'll comment on this after I finish reading it. (I get the impression that you are smiling and nodding agreement.)

But I have to tell you that reading all those books ever since I wrote *Healing with Padre Pio* has really consolidated my spiritual perspective on life, and I'm almost where I want to be in terms of my sense of personal comfort with respect to my knowledge of the perennial philosophy of life—meaning, my knowledge of the Way as it is being expressed in contemporary, especially cutting edge thought; and I'm happy to tell you that despite the brilliance and novelty of some of these cutting edge spiritual perspectives, I'm still very comfortable with mine because it adds something that all the other perspectives have yet to realize—the individuation of the "I" of God which resolves the paradox of the individual self and the universal Self. But that's enough for now. I just wanted to share my birthday gift with you.

I remain, in Spirit,
Orest

24. *Waiting for the Hour of New Clarity*

Monday, July 29, 2013

Dear Padre,

I was reading *Frequency, The Power of Personal Vibration* by Penny Peirce, this morning when I came across a quote from the poet Rainer Maria Rilke that jumped out at me: *"Fear not the strangeness you feel. The future must enter you long before it happens. Just wait for the birth, for the hour of new clarity."* That's what I'm waiting for!

I've been having moments of strange insight; moments when I am talking with someone (someone who needs a healing, though they may not know it), and I get these moments of surprising clarity that give me a glimpse into their life that allows me to say just what they need to hear to heal their wounded soul. It happened again Saturday evening when Penny and I went for dinner at a friend's house.

She invited us for dinner to thank us for listening to her situation at work, which she did not know how to handle. When we talked about her situation I had one of these moments of clarity and she heard exactly what she needed to hear to help her work out her situation; and over the thank-you dinner I had another moment of clarity which opened the door for her to hear what she needed to hear to further help heal her wounded soul.

So, what's going on here Padre? I got the impression when I talked with our friend Saturday evening that you whispered into my ear that I am becoming a teacher and a healer; is that what's going on? Am I becoming a teacher and a healer?

I don't mean to become a teacher and healer; it seems to be the outgrowth of the natural flow of my personal frequency, if I may use the term. So if I am becoming a teacher and healer, I am doing so in spite of myself. What does that sound like to you?

If you don't mind, I'd like to have a little dialogue with you; on paper, as it were. I am going to just let go and let be...

"Am I becoming a teacher and healer, in spite of myself?"

"*Yes. You have entered into a new phase of your life. It started with the spiritual healing that you recorded in your novel Healing with Padre Pio.*"

"Speaking of my novel, is it ever going to connect with my potential readers?"

"*Your impatience can be trying. Yes, it is; but only when you are ready to meet your public. And you know what I mean by this.*"

"Yes, I do; and I think this will be next summer. Right?"

"*Next summer will be your take-off point. You will have maxed out on your research for the next few books that you will be writing, and you will be connecting with your readers in the process of writing these books. It will change your life."*

"I don't want to hear that unless it's going to happen. I've hung my hat on that hope far too long, and if anything is boring—it's that!"

"Understood. But just wait and see. I don't make promises lightly, and I have made a promise to see you out there in print for the world to read your books. This is part of my mission from here, to get the word out that there is more than one way to God."

"Speaking of ways to God, I'm in a bit of a quandary with something that has come up with my research. I've been reading Ken Wilber lately, and I'm in a bit of a fog with respect to this concept of one Self that he espouses. I talked this over with you, and we both agreed upon the concept of life being a journey to the selfless self; is that not what we did?"

"Yes. And your concern is that your concept of the selfless self may be absorbed by the concept of the one Self theory?"

"In essence, yes. But I simply cannot allow that to happen because I know what I have experienced, and it is the natural flow of the frequency of my life—i. e., my personal journey from the self to the selfless self, which was your journey as well."

"And still is. There is no end to the journey of the selfless self. You are on the path that expresses your relationship with God. Wilber is on his path. The two paths don't negate each other, though he believes that

they do. You have to point this out in your writing, which you are doing with your spiritual musings. Don't be afraid. The Light shines through you in accordance to your need. When you need more, it will shine. That is what I am here for, to see you to your... realization. I couldn't think of the word, but that will do."

"This brings me to the point of this letter: when is the hour of my clarity going to visit me? And I don't mean little moments of clarity. I mean *the* hour of my clarity, the quantum leap into the "realization" of my personal frequency?"

"It's in the process. As we speak, the hour approaches. As I have already told you, just do what you are doing; the rest will take care of itself."

"What do you think of my book *The Summoning of Noman?*"

"A great insight into your parallel life. Well done. Let it sit for a few more months before you edit it. It will be one of your best books."

"And my novel *Tea with Grace?*"

"This one will connect. I would suggest you seek a mainstream publisher for this novel. It will speak to many, many readers. I will guide you on this."

"How?"

"That is for me to know. Just do what you feel you have to do, and let the universe unfold as it should. You are very much in your frequency, and you will be much more in your frequency when you begin working on your next book."

"Should I send inquiry emails for my novel *Tea with Grace*?"

"*Yes. Seek out publishers that have published similar books and send them an inquiry email, plus a sample chapter or two. You might be surprised.*"

"Do you mind communicating with me this way?"

"*Why should I? You have come a long way since your healing. Your mind is not as cluttered as it used to be. This is because you have transcended yourself.*"

"I'm overwhelmed by my research. What can I do to overcome that?"

"*You need not be afraid. Your path is solid. It is unique, and very different from the path of everyone you are researching. You will add much to their understanding. It is you that will be doing the intimidating, though not deliberately. The nature of your path is such that it stands alone in the history of personal paths. It is not unlike my path, but you have exteriorized it where I interiorized it. I am proud of you.*"

"Thank you, Padre. You have given me more comfort than anyone I know. And had it not been for you, I know that I'd be still behind the eight ball with my vanity."

"*Well put. But that's water under the bridge. Now you must concentrate on the next chapter of your life— the karma-free chapter. This is your mission in life, to introduce the world to the path of the karma-free life. This is all you need to know for today.*"

"Okay. I understand. Thank you, and until the next time..."

I remain,
Your faithful companion,
Orest

25. *My Exceptional Birthday Gift*

Wednesday, July 31, 2013

Dear Padre,

Today is my birthday. Fittingly, though I don't know why I say this, I just finished reading the last chapter of the best love story that I have ever read; not that I have read a lot of love stories. It would be more correct to say one of the best stories of love that I have ever read. Even that doesn't do it justice. It'll come to me as I write this. But if it comes or not, I can say that this book was an exceptional birthday gift.

The book is called *Grace and Grit*, by Ken Wilber; and it's the story of his love for Terry Killam and her love for him and their journey together through her five year ordeal with cancer—*it just came to me! Grace and Grit* is one of the best spiritual stories that I have ever read, the story of two souls in search of their heart center and divine consciousness; a story of recovery from all of life's vicissitudes. It made me cry.

My first impression upon completing this story is that LOVE IS THE WAY. No matter which path we take in life, it all comes down to love. Each and every path comes down to love in the end, and it would be wise to start with love to avoid all the heartache that comes with searching for the right path home to God. Just like you said, Padre: *"Learn to love what you do, and do what* you love; that's the sum of all spiritual paths that will take you to the Heart of God and happiness"

It does the soul good to read this book. It takes you through life's journey with such vicarious intensity that it makes you stop and reflect upon your own life. Ken and Treya (Terry changed her name to Treya, which is short for the Spanish word Estrella, which means star) have embraced the virtue of all spiritual paths, so their spiritual journey makes no distinctions per say; they speak from the heart, which is the true path. And speaking from the heart, they touch everyone with their story. That's why *Grace and Grit* has become the iconic love story that it has. And yet; and yet...

Okay, Padre; now we come to the heart of the matter (as if there could possibly be a heart of the matter, given the realization that the heart is the true path which *Grace and Grit* so profoundly illustrates). Nonetheless, the heart of the matter for me is this...I don't quite know how to put it to words, so I'm just going to dive in and let go—

Grace and Grit brought to my awareness as no other book has the distinction between the WAY OF BEING and THE WAY OF NON-BEING. I don't know if I should go into this now, probably because I want to do a spiritual musing on this insight; but I have to get in on record now that *Grace and Grit* is a story about the WAY OF NON-BEING.

It's definitely a story of the heart, a story of love, compassion, surrender, and acceptance; but it is a story of the WAY OF NON-BEING; and by this I mean that it is a story of Soul's journey of spiritual self-realization through the consciousness of non-being.

Because Ken and Treya embraced the one Self view of life, their spiritual journey reflects the reality of overcoming the ego to realize the Universal Self; and this journey is distinct from the WAY OF BEING, which speaks to the journey of what I can only call the divination of the self—the journey of the individual self to the Divine Self.

The distinction then between the two ways is this: THE WAY OF NON-BEING is a journey through the non-reality of the transitory ego self; and the WAY OF BEING is a journey through the individuation of the divine Soul self.

The WAY OF NON-BEING does not embrace the reality of the individual self, and the WAY OF BEING embraces the reality of the individual self; but both ways lead to the God Self—the Divine I Am Principle of life.

I don't know how else to express this now, Padre; but I know that this distinction exists, because I have worked my way through the non-being of my life to center myself in the being of my life, and like you I know that life is a journey of the self—that distinct, individual spark of God that we came into this world to realize.

We all came as God seeds, and our divine purpose in life is to grow and evolve in our own unique nature until we become aware of our own divinity, or God Self if you will; and there are two ways to do this—the WAY OF BEING and THE WAY OF NON-BEING; and *Grace and Grit* is a love story of two souls that have chosen to work their way to God through the consciousness of non-being. *A wonderful, wonderful story!*

I must thank Penny for my exceptional birthday gift.

Until again,
Your faithful companion,
Orest

26. *The Vicissitudes of Life*

Saturday, August 3, 2013

Dear Padre,

We got a call yesterday from one of our tenants who has been living in our triplex up north for the past nine years that she will be leaving at the first of next month; she's going to be moving into a nursing home in Thunder Bay. We are sorry to lose her.

I took the blow very hard last night when she called. I went into semi-panic mode, because we pay our mortgage for our triplex with the income from our tenants. We have two tenants left, and one of them is a senior also who may also be ready for a nursing home. We don't know how long she is going to be with us. I hope for this winter at least. And our third tenant is not that reliable for monthly payments. He's always got excuses, and we've been very lenient with him. He's two months behind in his rent. So Padre, what to do?

I should have listened to Penny years ago and put the house up for sale, and I honestly don't know why I didn't. The market in our hometown is depressed, and I know that we would take a loss on our house; and the house needs some work.

I guess we'll start by advertising a vacant apartment and hope we can occupy it for the winter at least. I don't want to see it empty for the winter. I'm going to ask for your help, Padre. Get us a new tenant, or maybe someone interested in buying our house; the latter would be preferable. I ask, because I don't think I can take the pressure.

Let me explain. Ever since my bypass operation I have lost my nerve. This is not easy for me to confess, but I don't have the internal fortitude to withstand the pressures of life like I used to, because I know that I can't get myself out of life's predicaments with my body anymore because I can't work. My work was my salvation. I could always rely on my body to do the work necessary to survive, but I can't work with my body like I could before my heart operation, and I go into panic mode whenever a crisis comes up.

I know that losing a tenant isn't that big a crisis, but for me it is; and I felt the effect that it had on my body last night. I felt sick. I'm only a little bit better today, but I'm still in fear of what could happen. Oh God, why couldn't I have taken care of Penny better? Why didn't I concentrate on saving for retirement? Why was I driven the way I was to find the Way and work the answer to my haunting question—who am I?

I don't want to go into a big whine here, Padre. I could easily, but I just don't want to go there because I don't like feeling sorry for myself. As I was waiting for my coffee this morning I thought of what would have happened if Penny and I didn't move down this way, if I would not have written those two books that forced us to relocate because they offended the people of my hometown, and the truth is that I wouldn't have had my seven past life regressions down here, I wouldn't have worked out the Divine Plan of God, I wouldn't have met you Padre, and I wouldn't have written all those books which have opened the door for so much more spiritual growth; so as painful as it was to move here, had we stayed up north our life would have been entirely different, and I know that I would never have been given a glimpse of the divine mysteries that I was given here in Georgian Bay.

I guess what I'm trying to say is that for all of the vicissitudes of our life, things always seemed to turn out for the best; and I hope this new vicissitude will bring a new and better change. I do have a few more books to write, Padre. One more with you, in fact; and I don't want to have to live under financial pressure. My heart can't take it.

God, that was hard for me to say! Why is it so hard for me to admit my vulnerability? I tell you, I could rely on my body before. My whole life my body was my strength, but now that I can't rely on my body for work I feel so damn vulnerable. I just don't know what I can do to make things better. I write, hoping that one of my books is going to connect; but nothing seems to be happening. You said three years and something would happen with *Healing with Padre Pio*; well, I think we're going into the third year soon, and I sure hope that something happens. It sure would take the pressure off if it connected.

In a word, I'm vulnerable today and I'm asking for an intervention. Could you please help correct this new little vicissitude that has befallen us? I want so much for Penny and I to go into our senior years with grace and dignity. It means the world to me.

In gratitude,
Your faithful companion,
Orest

27. Yesterday's Folly

Thursday, August 28, 2013

Dear Padre,

Am I going to be defeated by my own smallness? Have I come this far only to fall into the small world of my little self?

I am so tired of nothing happening after all the work that I have put into my books. I want to leave and take a limitless holiday from myself. I am at the beach listening to the waves break upon the shore. The sound is soothing. I am going to lie down on this bench and listen to the waves. I need to heal myself.

I am so tired, Padre. I need to rest myself. I can no longer abide the vanity. It terrifies me to feel that I may go to the other side feeling like I have failed to make a difference. This is sad. The depths of my vanity continue to haunt me. I fear I am doomed to obscurity despite my best efforts. I have one request: liberate me from my dreams.

Gratefully yours,
Orest

28. *Another Day*

Dear Padre,

I'm getting tired of all my research reading. I think I am going to take a break from that kind of reading and do some short story and novel reading.

Yesterday was a rough day. It began with my dreams. I hate some of my dreams, and I would like to be liberated from them. I don't want to talk about them, but you know which ones they are; and especially my hometown dreams. Why do I keep going back there in my dreams, anyway? And why cannot I ever dream about my life as a writer?

I spent the best energies of my life writing, why cannot I have dreams that have to do with writing? I find that so strange that it annoys me. It's as though this part of my life, which is the biggest part, doesn't exist in my dream world; and that's so frustrating that I just don't know what to make of it. Can you give me some clarity on this, Padre?

I just finished editing "my forgotten novel" *Tea with Grace*. Penny created the book cover, and we hope to have it out this fall. Maybe this one will connect with the reader. I hope so, because like I said yesterday, I'm tired of waiting.

Penny and I were sitting on the deck after dinner last night and I said to her that I feel like I have fallen into oblivion. I've always felt that I was relevant, but this feeling of falling into oblivion has deprived me of my feeling of relevance, and it is frightening.

"I'm just like everybody else now," I said. I didn't mean that in a negative way; I meant that I've always felt that I was born to some destined purpose, but this feeling of slipping into oblivion has eroded my sense of destined purpose and I am just like everyone else now, and that's a scary feeling.

It's scary because I've always felt myself to be different. It was this feeling of being different that fueled my life, and now it has worn so thin that I am slipping into oblivion, and it leaves me feeling like I have failed my life.

Is that it? Is that what I'm feeling, my own failure. It has never occurred to me that I would ever fail in my destined purpose, but now it has snuck up on me and I can feel its presence. It hasn't quite got me yet, but I can feel its presence. I don't want to dwell on it for fear of giving it more life than it already has, so I am going to drop the subject.

On with today. I'm going to read *Tea with Grace* one more time before I turn the manuscript over to Penny, and then I can concentrate on my next book. I think it's going to be my novel *The Gnostic Master*. I've got it started. About one third done. That's all I can do. Just keep on butting my head against that invisible wall...

I feel that I have to get back in touch with myself. When I lose touch with myself I lose contact with the source and my life begins to dry up. I hate it when my life starts to dry up. I have to get back into the flow. I have to take my finger out of the hole in the tree of my dream that is the source of the living water of my life. But how do I do that?

I have to reconnect with myself, Padre; that's what I heard you say to me just now. I have to find the source of my reconnection. Journal writing is one of the best ways to reconnect with myself. Reading poetry. And doing my spiritual contemplation. And, let me not forget, DOING my household duties.

God, I hate myself for being such a procrastinator! Am I destined to go out of this life putting things off? I'm such a procrastinator that I may just not go at all! That's how entrenched I am in my procrastination! Stuck between knowing what I have to do and putting off what I have to do—the guilt is drying me up!

Is that the source of my dryness? Have I stumbled upon the secret of my shadow's hold upon me? Wow! That's way too much for one day...

Until the next time,
Orest

29. *Running on Empty*

Dear Padre,

I had a strange experience yesterday, Friday 13th. I was doing the third edit of my new book of spiritual musings (*Stupidity Is Not a Gift of God*) when I got a call from Penny from Wal-Mart where she was doing her Hallmark Card work. It was about ten thirty and a little early for her call. She wanted to know if I was going out.

I said that perhaps I could meet her for coffee at the McDonald's restaurant in Wal-Mart; so after I finished editing the spiritual musing that I was working on, I got into my van and drove into Wasaga Beach to meet Penny.

As I was driving I noticed that I was low on gas, so I decided to get gas before going to Wal-Mart. There was a little Esso Gas Service Bar next to Coffee Time, just across the street from Wal-Mart where I often got gas, which was rather handy; but when I was driving down Concession Ten, about half way to Wasaga, my low gas light came on.

I didn't think I was that low on gas because the needle showed just a little below the quarter full mark, but I felt I had enough to get to the Beach; which I did. I pulled into the little Esso Gas Bar and got out to put gas into my van, but then I noticed that the little booth where the gas attendant served his customers was empty. He place was shut down.

He had gone out of business, so I got into my van to drive to another station in the Beach where I also gassed up; but my van wouldn't start. "Oh no," I said.

I didn't have enough gas in the van for it to turn over. I tried two or three more times, but my motor wouldn't kick in. Pausing for a moment to collect myself, I thought about what could be wrong. Was I just out of gas, or was it something else?

I turned the key two more times, but the motor wouldn't start; so I got out and walked across to Wal-Mart to see Penny, whom I had started calling my "go-to person" because she solves all of my computer kinks. She suggested we buy a small gas can in the store and get gas and try the van; so that's what we did.

I bought a small gas can and Penny drove me over to the Pioneer Gas Service Bar just up the street and I got ten dollars' worth of gas, but when I finally managed to get gas into my van (the spout was too short, but I finally made it work), I made a quick invocation to Divine Spirit asking for assistance, and my van started. Thank goodness.

Padre, I had all kinds of fears that it was more than an empty gas tank; so I was ready to have it towed to a service station. But thankfully it was just an empty gas tank. The van is getting old, and I don't know how much longer it's going to last (I had a motor job done on it several years ago), so the thought crossed our mind to take on a new lease payment for a new vehicle rather than pour more money into my van; but the van seemed to be okay, and I didn't' stop to have coffee with Penny. I thanked and kissed her for her help, and I drove back home and made myself lunch and went back to work on my manuscript.

So, Padre; what does that mean? Don't you find it rather strange that I make it all the way to my little Esso Gas Bar only to find out that it went out of business? And that I could not get my van started to go to another station because I didn't have enough gas to turn the motor over? What was the language of life telling me?

Coincidentally enough, I was reading a book on the language of life before I got into my manuscript, a book called *The Waking Dream* by Ray Grasse, which explored the symbolist view of the world; meaning, the belief that all of Nature speaks to us through signs and symbols, which the ancients and some primitive cultures today knew how to read, and which Carl Jung began to explore again through his study of myths and the phenomenon that he called "synchronicity."

I believe in the language of life, and I'm always reading the signs and symbols; that's why I wonder what it meant for me to pull my van into a gas station that had gone out of business. My van was too low on gas to turn the motor over, and I was inconvenienced by having to buy a gas can and get gas at another station to get my van started.

Thank God it started. Then I drove my van to the Pioneer Gas Bar (with Penny following me just in case) and put another twenty-five dollars of gas into the van, and then, as I said, I thanked Penny and drove home. So, what did that all mean?

What was the message of this curious incident?

Don't let my tank get so low on gas? Metaphorically, does this mean that I should be more attentive to my personal energy level? That I should be more disciplined in my spiritual contemplations? Which reminds me of a talk given by the Spiritual Leader of the Way of the Eternal which he titled "Gas or God?"

I think the language of life was telling me that I have to not let my "personal tank" get so low on energy. That's it. Whatever else the language of life was trying to tell me, I'll have to wait and see if it will disclose its deeper message...Could it be that the publication of *Stupidity Is Not a Gift of God* is going to replenish my "personal tank"?

Wouldn't that be nice!

Ciao for now,
Your faithful companion,
Orest

30. *The Root Cause of Depression*

Friday, November 1, 2013

Dear Padre,

I'm hesitant to write. I have started two or three spiritual musings, but I couldn't get past the first few paragraphs. I put them aside and lost the poignancy of the creative impulse that inspired the musings; and now they sit in the shop of my mind like partially-built furniture waiting forlornly to be completed. It makes me sad.

I feel like I am slowly betraying myself. The more I distance myself from my writing, the more I feel like I have betrayed myself. Like I am running away from what I have been called to do, and be; and I can feel a mild state of depression setting in.

This is curious, because Penny's friend was here visiting for the weekend (she was in Toronto for a nursing seminar and came for a visit before returning home), and we were talking about her spouse's depression. He's off work again, and this concerned her; so we talked about the causes of depression.

I told her that as much as I believed that depression has a chemical component, I firmly believe that depression is essentially psychological; a state brought on by one's unresolved conflicts. I honestly believe depression is shadow related, and the best cure for that would be to confront one's shadow and integrate it through effort. This would require shadow work, which can be found in Jungian therapy. And the root cause of one's depression can be found in one's self-betrayal. I'm convinced of that.

That's why I feel this mild state of depression is setting in on me, because I am not being true to myself. I am avoiding doing what I am meant to do, which is to write; this is why I decided to write you a letter this morning. I want to reconnect with my creative self so I can reaffirm myself and get back on track—

"What do you think, Padre?"

"I think you are doing the right thing. Take your time. Do not rush into it. Just work your way into it gradually. You have recognized the central problem that people have to face in their life, which is personal honesty. When a person begins to lose their sense of personal honesty, they disconnect with their inner self; and it is this disconnect that brings on the state of depression. Now that you recognize it, you can move on. You were meant to recognize it, after offering your advice so freely to Penny's friend—"

"Alright. I get it. You don't have to rub it in. I got a taste of what he's going through, and now I can move on. But if I may, let's continue this. I have much more I would like to discuss with you, if you don't mind.""

"I don't mind. I have been waiting patiently for you to contact me. There is much you have to learn yet, but you learn by doing; so get back to your writing. Writing is your process. Writing connects you with the creative life force, and this nourishes your soul with the Light of God. It is your way. What is it you wish to ask me?"

"My first question is this: I am coming to the stark realization that I am coming to the end of the road with respect to my research reading, and I want to know if this is true or not because I have the strongest feeling that wants to possess me that I have to write to get the answers that I am looking for; am I right in this feeling?"

"Yes. You have all you need to write what you have to write. You will continue to read for research, but you will be reading with less intensity because you no longer need to know anything more to do your writing. You have all the information you need for the next books that you are going to write."

"I have been putting this off for some time now, but I honestly feel that I can't put it off any longer: I FEEL COMPELLED TO WRITE CREATIVE FICTION. SHORT STORIES, NOVELLAS, AND NOVELS. Am I correct in this feeling?"

"You could not be more correct. It is through the creative process of story writing that you will shine in your craft. You will prove to be the writer that you have always wanted to be when you first got the inspiration to become a writer. This is why you have gone back to your literary mentor Ernest Hemingway. He is still your inspiration. Yes, by all means go back to story writing.

Do not forsake your musings. They are your intellectual discipline, and they will serve their literary purpose as well. But your creative stories will be the mark that you will leave behind. They will be your legacy to the world."

"Like my novel *Tea with Grace?*"

"Absolutely. You have no idea how proud I am of you for writing this novel. It speaks to the issue of Christianity with a narrative clarity that defies categorization. It is truly a work of art. You have done the novel proud."

"That's why I've been hesitant to jump back in. I feel that I may not do the genre the justice it deserves. It feels like I have fallen off the horse and don't want to get back on; but I have to, because the call is too strong. IT'S SHOUTING AT ME!"

"I'm shouting at you. I want you to get back onto your horse. You have so many good stories in you and you have to get them out. It's in the story that the message lies. Trust the creative process. It will serve you well, in more ways than one."

"And all of my other worries?"

"Let me take care of them for you. Just do what you have been called to do. That's what your duty must be. WRITE, and let the story out."

"I'm torn between working on my novel *The Gnostic Master* or work on some new stories. They seem to be working their way to the surface of my mind. What do you think I should do? Novel or short stories?"

"It doesn't matter which you work on, they will all be written eventually. If you feel that you would like to start fresh with a new story, then go with it because it will excite your creative imagination to write something new. Trust your Muse, as you say."

"One more fear that has to be addressed. I am beginning to hear time's winged chariot drawing near. Will I have enough time to write what I am called to write?"

"Yes. And now plan your day and begin. That's all for now."

"Thank you, Padre."

"You're welcome. If I may, just let your mind go blank whenever your thoughts turn to worries. Raise yourself above them. Practice your old discipline of non-identification. It is a perfect discipline for what ails you. Have a wonderful day, my friend."

"I will, and thank you again Padre."

As always,
Your faithful companion,
Orest

31. *The Consciousness of Poverty, and the Poverty of Consciousness*

Saturday, November 9, 2013

Dear Padre,

It started with Joe Fiorito's memoir, *The Closer We Are to Dying*; the story of his relationship with his father who's in the hospital dying of cancer.

Why I was strongly nudged to read this book, I don't know; but one day last week I "felt" like checking out the bottom shelf of my bookcase beside my recliner in the sun room, and I spotted Fiorito's book which I purchased a couple of years ago because Joe Fiorito was born and raised in Thunder Bay, which I know very well because I grew up in Nipigon just an hour's drive away and I went to university in Thunder Bay; and Penny and I did our shopping there and often went out for dinner and a movie in the city.

The Closer We Are to Dying is a moving and courageous memoir. Joe Fiorito's style is journalistic, not unlike Ernest Hemingway's lean, evocative style. His short, punchy sentences grab your attention, and he knows how to weave a story; but what fascinated me was that familiar southern Italian consciousness that spoke to my life.

I was born in Calabria, southern Italy; and being Calabrese, I'm very familiar with what I now call that consciousness of poverty that shaped my life. That's why Fiorito's book spoke to me, because it revealed just how much that consciousness of poverty had shaped his family's life, which he was struggling to understand.

Joe Fiorito is puzzled by his father the mailman and amateur musician and singer with a short temper that terrorized his family while he was growing up. He has a love-hate relationship with Dusty Fiorito, and as he sits vigil by his father's bedside he weaves the raw, naked story of their conflicted relationship hoping that by writing about it he will come to a better understanding of his father, and his own life.

Writing always brings more clarity to a subject, and by focusing on his father with his gift for writing, I think Joe succeeded. He got to frame Dusty Fiorito's life in the context of his full life that went way back to his family roots in that poverty-stricken part of Italy which inspired my father's favorite curse, *"Mannaga la miseria!"*

In the words of the American poet Adrienne Rich, Joe Fiorito transformed the reality of his relationship with his father into a deeper perception by writing about it, and he came out of his book feeling much more resolved and at peace with himself.

I was so moved by *The Closer We Are to Dying* that I dug up another book that I had intended to read but never got around to it because it wasn't meant to be read at the time, *Women of the Shadows, A Study of the Wives and Mothers of Southern Italy,* by Ann

Cornelisen; and once I got into it I couldn't stop until I finished it.

I don't quite know how to express this, Padre; but not until I read Joe Fiorito's book and Ann Cornelisen's memoir of her twenty years of living in the poverty-stricken villages of southern Italy did I finally come to understand why I had such an insatiable hunger for knowledge growing up, and why I couldn't read enough books to satisfy my ravenous hunger—*it was because I was born with a hole in my soul!*

This hole in my soul was genetic. That's the only way I can describe it, because my parents were born and raised in a consciousness of poverty that bred a poverty of consciousness that was passed on to their children as inherent ignorance, which I can only describe as a hole in my soul that I could not fill no matter how many books I read; but it goes much deeper than that, Padre. Much, much deeper...

I don't want to explore this today. I may explore it in another letter, or a spiritual musing; for now, all I want to say is that my self-sabotaging impoverished southern Italian family consciousness was responsible for our devastating family shadow, which was the bane of my life; but, paradoxically, without the richness of my family shadow I wouldn't have had the pathological drive to go on my quest for my true self. *What irony!*
Ciao for now,
Your fellow companion,
Orest

32. *Innocent Perception*

Dear Padre,

I'm in a strange place. How many times have I said this? Well, I am. I feel like my cup of learning is overflowing. I'm saturated. I can't seem to take in any more knowledge, and I feel like the stupidest man in the world. Why the paradox, Padre?

"Knowledge is exponential. The more you know, the more you realize there is to know; and this can overwhelm you. It is only natural. But this too shall pass."

I don't want to get into this form of dialogue. I don't want to lean on you in this way; at least, not at this time. I want to wrestle my way through this rut I'm in. So, if you don't mind, I'm going to ramble until I get to the bottom of this issue.

As much as I hate to admit this, I'm afraid to write something new. I don't seem to have that connection that gave me the inspiration to jump into a new project; and the more I put it off, the more afraid I am to jump in. This is strange for me.

The idea for a short book came to me yesterday morning. The title came to me also: *Do We Have an Immortal Soul?* I started the first paragraph, but I don't know if it's the right point of entry. I have to wait and see. I'm afraid to jump in.

The idea for this book came to me after watching a You Tube video of Brother Wayne Teasdale and Ken Wilber. They both held the view that we don't have an autonomous self. That we are all one Universal Self. I don't disagree; but that does not negate the existence of our autonomous self. That's what I wanted to explore in my little book, which would really be a long, personal essay.

What do you think, Padre; should I explore this question?

"It is a worthy subject. It would help clear the issue for your reader. It is still an issue for many people, and if you could help to clarify it for them you would be doing a great service to the world. It's entirely up to you."

Of course it is. That's the point of this letter, isn't it? I'm having trouble jumping into my project. I think I have to find my way again. I feel I have lost it. Not entirely, but lost enough for me to experience the anxiety of getting lost.

That's what's bothering me. I fear the anxiety of losing my way. I know I would never lose my way, because I am my own Way; I know that, but it is frightening knowing that I've come this far only to realize that I know so little. Why the quest, then?

"As you have written, you have to become to realize that you are. That's why."

"Why are we dialoguing this way?"

"You insist on getting answers, because they're not coming from within you. All you have to do is dig deeper. Go to your source."

"Which is?"

"Innocent perception, as you read this morning in The Keys of Jeshua."

"This is what you are referring to: 'When you can live each day as if it were your first and only day, you will enjoy innocent perception.' Jeshua (Jesus) said that to Glenda Green, the artist who painted the portrait of Jesus and wrote *Love without End, Jesus Speaks* and *The Keys of Jeshua* which I was reading this morning.

"I think I understand what you are telling me: I have to let go of what I know and just BE what I am. BEING, not knowing is where I will find the answer to my quandary. I have to just BE ME. Is that what you are telling me?"

"Precisely. This will take you out of your slump. Just BE. This will kick up the Nike saying (Just do it!) up a notch. Don't think so much. Just BE, and then do!"

"In other words, abandon to the creative spirit and jump in; is that it?"

"Yes."

"Enough said. I can take it from here. I want to bring up another matter, seemingly unrelated but completely relevant. Brother Wayne Teasdale and Ken Wilber were rather snide about Neale Donald Walsh and his little book industry based on his conversations with God. I found their attitude rather small for such enlightened beings. Personally, I like Walsh's books, and I like him. I've seen his interviews, and he comes across to me like an honest, genuine person. He's authentic, and I resonate with what he says."

"Because you have both suffered. That is your bond. You both understand the ways of the heart. This was his connection with God. This is why God spoke to him. We know God to be his Higher Self, but what does it matter what we call it? Like you say, it is the gems of wisdom that come through that is important."

"Why the resentment from Brother Teasdale and Wilber?"

"They are what they are. In time, they too will appreciate that there is more than one way. This is not the easiest lesson in the world to learn, despite how enlightened one may be. There are many forms of enlightenment, but this is subject for another time."

"Fair enough. So, thank you Padre. All I have to do is stop thinking about my project, as such; just BE, and Do! Actually, this is what Jeshua said. If I may, let me quote the passage that I read this morning: 'When you say YOU ARE, then you BECOME...not the other way around. All of man's illumined realizations begin as innocent perceptions. One's learning progresses by way of simple verifiable perceptions. If complex concepts are to be taught, they must be reduced to simple images that are universal in meaning. For that reason, I often spoke in parables—they contain a spark of timeless truth that adapts to the moment, place, and person.'" (*The Keys of Jeshua*, p. 70)

"That's clear enough. Just remind yourself to be as a child; that way you will stay in that mode of innocent perception which will keep away your fear of not knowing."

"Well, I got my answer; didn't I? I went into this letter with an issue about my fear of starting a new project, and I got the answer to not think about it. Just BE, and jump into the project; because in BEING, I put myself into that state of innocent perception which opens me up to the entire consciousness of I AM, and that removes all fear of not knowing. Is that what it all comes down to, Padre? Just BE, and let the knowing take care of itself?"

"In essence, yes; that's the answer for your quandary."

"One more thing before I close off. Why did I slip into this mode of communicating with you?"

"You have a natural tendency to trust your Muse, which as you correctly say is Divine Spirit. Knowing that I am one with Divine Spirit, you are open to this form of communication. Do not be afraid of it. It is a safe way to grow and understand. But for now, do not lean upon it too much. Lean upon your own creative spirit."

"I understand, because the more I lean upon my own creative spirit the more I am drawing upon Divine Spirit; isn't that so?"

"See what I mean? You have a wisdom that needs to be expressed. Just BE, and DO; that should be your motto. Is there anything else?"

"Not for now. Thank you, Padre."

"You're welcome. Have a wonderful and creative day. Ciao."

Ciao,
Your faithful companion,
Orest

33. *Do We Have an Immortal Soul?*

Saturday, January 4, 2014

Dear Padre,

Well, here I am; back from my foray into the far country of my life—that wonderful world of creative expression with my new book *Do We Have an Immortal Soul?* that I brought to closure on December 25, 2013; which I found rather delightful, like it was a Christmas gift from my higher Self. To be honest, I didn't expect to bring it to closure on Christmas day; but all the pieces fell into place and I KNEW it was finished.

I've been meaning to write you sooner, and I did try several times to drop you a line; but for one reason or another, I didn't finish my letter. So I just deleted what I started, and maybe down the road I can share with you what I had in mind at the time—like the little incident that Penny had a few weeks ago that I saw as a "waking dream. Maybe I can share that with you now....

I gave Penny my third volume of spiritual musings to edit. It's called *Stupidity Is Not a Gift of God.* It is a very powerful book, and Penny could only read a few chapters at a time because it was too much for her to take in all at once.

Well, she did finish editing the book; and I asked her what she thought. She replied something to the effect that it expanded her mind, giving her a different perspective on life. Then the following day or the day after she was doing some dusting in her bedroom and she dropped a little glass lamp that we have on the dresser table in case the power goes out. I heard the noise from my writing den and asked her what happened. She told me, and it didn't take long for me to see that as a waking dream.

A waking dream is an experience that happens in our everyday waking life that is out of the ordinary; and breaking a glass lamp is out of the ordinary.

Why did it slip from her hand and fall and break? Was her creative unconscious trying to tell her something? I think so. That's why I called it a waking dream; and here's my explanation: I think that *Stupidity Is Not a Gift of God* forced Penny to have a paradigm shift in consciousness; from lesser awareness to more awareness of how the life process works. In effect, her old lamp for seeing the world broke because now she had a new, brighter lamp to see the world. That's why I called her experience a waking dream.

What do you think, Padre?

Anyway, back to my new book. The idea came to me one morning a couple of months ago when Penny and I were having our morning coffee in my writing den, and I worked on it every day until I finished on Christmas Day.

I know you were standing over me as I wrote it, because it tells the story of how I came to the realization that we are all born as sparks of divine consciousness. I printed out a copy yesterday for Penny to read and edit, and then we will see about publishing it.

Oh, I was nudged to send a letter of inquiry to PARABOLA magazine this morning to see if they would be interested in publishing one of the chapters of my new book, called "The Creative Unconscious." It has to do with SYNCHRONCITY.

It would be nice if they are interested. Why don't you use some of that high-powered influence that you have and help get me out there? At this stage of the game, I'm not beyond asking for help. In any event, I'm going to publish my little book *Do We Have an Immortal Soul* because it's meant to be out there; otherwise I wouldn't have been so strongly nudged to write it.

That's all for now. Until the next time,

Ciao,
Your faithful companion,
Orest

34. *Artists Know the Meaning and Purpose of Life*

Monday, January 6, 2014

Dear Padre,

I'm stuck in that old familiar place between **doing** and **non-doing**, that evil place that Jesus referred to when he said *"But let your communication be, Yae, yae: Nay; nay; for whatsoever is more than these cometh of evil"* (Math. 5: 37); and by this I mean that I'm between writing projects, and I feel—yes, in a sense, evil.

What a curious thing. Why would I feel "evil" because I'm not "communicating," as Jesus would say? Writing is communicating, is it not? And when I'm not writing I feel like I'm wasting my day—*just as Doris Lessing realized!*

What a curious coincidence. Last night I watched an online video interview of Doris Lessing, who won the Nobel Prize for Literature in 2007, and she revealed how she felt when she didn't write every day. She said she could be in her garden working, or doing whatever, but if she didn't write that day she felt she had wasted her day; like she wasn't being true to herself—which reminds me of a quote by the artist Pablo Picasso who said: *"The meaning of life is to find your gift. The purpose of life is to give it away."* In her own intuitive way, Doris Lessing reveals the moral imperative of Picasso's brilliant insight into the meaning and purpose of life.

I'd like to explore this. What do you say, Padre? Are you up to a little chat this morning? I mean a face to face, so to speak—or Soul to Soul. That would be more appropriate. Just to feel this thought out; an exercise in "active imagination", to use Jung's term for this kind of exercise in creative exploration—

"Personally, I think Picasso hit the nail on the head. He's referring to what I have come to recognize as the two destinies of man: our *karmic destiny*, and our *spiritual destiny*. We are free to choose our own life, but we are also destined by our spiritual DNA to realize our divine nature. So our **life-meaning** would be to realize our karmic destiny, which is the realization of the karmically evolved "gift" of our spiritual nature; and our **life-purpose** would be to share this "gift" with the world. What do you think?"

"*I think you are avoiding doing what you should be doing, if we are to be completely honest with ourselves.*"

"Alright, I get it. Just don't rub it in, please. I feel guilty enough as it is. I know I should be focusing my creative energies on stories of the heart, as you suggested in one of my spiritual healing sessions; but I have been productive. Why do I keep putting off my stories of the heart? Am I afraid to go there?"

"*Yes and no. You are much too preoccupied with getting your own spiritual quest out of the way, which is a good thing; but you fail to realize—or refuse to realize—that writing stories of the heart will be as effective, if not a hundred times more, than the simple prose narrative of your quest. Stories of the heart speak to people on an entirely different level of thought. They touch the heart, and that's what you have to concentrate on to maximize your talent; and you have developed quite a talent for expressing yourself. So try not to put it off too long. Before you know it, you may never get the chance. One story a month. That's all it takes. You did make a New Year's resolution to read one Alice Munroe story every week; now make a resolution to write a story of the heart every month—good, bad, or indifferent; just do it to build up the momentum for creative story writing, which will be your literary forte."*

"You can see it?"

"Of course."

"If I may take the liberty, what do you think of my new book, *Do We Have an Immortal Soul?*"

"It's going to take the world by storm. Give it a chance. Let the world find out about it through You Tube. You will be discovered online. Trust me, please."

"I don't know what to trust anymore. It's been such a long journey, especially since, as you told me, this is my second time around. I know I broke the karmic pattern of my life and slipped into a parallel universe, but it's still my life; and memories and dreams keep reminding me of my life before I entered into my parallel life, so I don't really know what to believe, or what to trust. It's all a big circle—"

"*It is a big circle, and the purpose and meaning of life is to complete the circle of your karmic patterns. You are perfectly correct to see life as a closed circuit, because that's exactly what it is; and finding a way to break the circuit is what the meaning and purpose of life comes down to. As you have reasoned, the karmic pattern can only be broken when you transcend your life; which is what your quest was all about in your parallel life. And you have written quite a record, which will benefit many, many souls when it is brought out to the world. DO NOT FRET. IT IS COMING!*"

"In my lifetime, or do I have to come back again into my same life to realize it? Which is a good question, isn't it? How many times can a soul be reborn into the same body? An infinite number of times?"

"*Theoretically, yes; but there have been cases of a soul being reborn into the same body up to four times. You are not one. This third time will be enough for you, because you managed to break the code, as you like to say.*"

"How about you? Didn't you break the code with the suffering of *la via di sofferenza*? All of your suffering transformed you into an angel of light, did it not?"

"*Yes, if you want to express it like that. My suffering was karmically destined; or, rather, I chose to take on the stigmata as my way to God.*"

"Did you ever return to your same body to live over again?"

"*Yes, but let's not go there. We are concentrating on your meaning and purpose, which is to fulfill your destiny in your parallel life. You have transcended the voice of your old life and have realized your OWN voice; which is your Soul Voice. This is the voice of all your lives, and you must learn to trust it. It has its own story, its own message, its own truth, its own frequency; and it is your job to express it in the best way possible, which is writing stories of the heart, because these are the stories that resonate most with the world. AND YOU WILL RESONATE. You must listen to the call, and just BE what you are now—a creative writer. This is your purpose. Alright. Get on with your day. We can continue this another time—"*

"Fair enough. Ciao for now, then."

"Ciao, my beloved friend."

"Thanks, Padre."

"You're welcome."

Until the next time,
Orest

35. *Padre Pio's Promise*

Sunday, January 12, 2014

Dear Padre,

I'm anxious, and I don't like the effect it's having on me. I could easily have a heart attack if this anxiety persists. It has to do with life-obligations, which I feel I cannot live up to because of my heart condition. I don't know if I am lying to myself, but I honestly feel overwhelmed by my life-obligations, starting with responsibilities to our triplex up north; things that have to be taken care of. So I'm writing to ask for your healing energy.

I'd like to lay down and translate to the other side. I can't, but I'd like to. I can't leave Penny. It's not fair to her. I have to see this life through. I'm here, with all my baggage, and I have to see it through. I've got twelve books published now, and as satisfying as this is I don't feel satisfied. I feel like I cheated Penny out of a better life because I devoted much too much time to my writing. I tried to split the energies between writing and my life obligations, but my split wasn't even; I gave too much to my writing.

My writing was the consequence of my spiritual quest, and I was driven to find my true self; but I gave way too much energy to my quest and my life with Penny suffered. I don't want to go too much in this vein because I don't want to guilt-trip myself with more guilt than I can suffer; but I am tired, Padre. I am tired of my life. I would like some respite. Oh God, would I like some respite just to experience some anxiety-free days; but will it ever come?

"Put your trust in the divine process," I hear you saying to me; and I know that you are right, that's what I should do. But how long do I have to wait?

I have laid my life on the line for what I found in my quest; I have bridged the great divide. You even said that you were "satisfied and content with what we have accomplished" with my novel *Healing with Padre Pio*; but life goes on in the same old anxiety-filled way, and I am tired in my soul. I know you know the feeling, because you carried your cross right to the end of your life. Well, I'm really tired too.

I thought of writing a story called *"La Nostra Via,"* making you a character in the story; a mysterious man who is and is not Padre Pio. I don't want to start it, because I feel that I would not be writing what I am called to write—personal stories; stories inspired by my own life experiences that need to be told, like *"The Sunworshipper."*

Padre, I need a huge infusion of healing energy. Is that possible? Can I call in some karma chips? I know I have a bundle of good karma stored up; can I call in some chips and get some respite? I need it badly.

"Open your heart to God's love and you will get all the respite you need. It is not that difficult. Whenever I was down in the dumps I prayed. You don't pray because

it is not in you to beg God for help; but you can open your heart to God and let God's love pour into you. That is the way of the open heart. Here's what you do: think of all the times you loved, and let your heart fill with those memories. Think of one time, one moment of love, and just let the love fill your heart again; that's the exercise. It is your prayer. Don't ask for anything more, because God's love is all there is. I am always with you, my dear friend."

"I know you are, but how easily I forget. I will think of the love-moments of my life, most of which were with Penny. But why do the anxiety moments pervade my mind?"

"It is the way of the body. The body is made of life's energy, and life's energy is an energy of coming and going. It's in the going energy that you get caught up in, and by this I mean the energy that cannot be. It is the energy of disintegration. It is the energy of transition, which pulls you into the state of consciousness of not being you. You have become you, and when you get caught up in thoughts that have not been harmoniously fused into who you are, all those anxiety moments as you call them, you feel the full weight of their incompleteness; and it is this incompleteness that bothers you. And the best way to overcome this false sense of incompleteness is to fill your mind with your heartfelt emotions of love, especially your love of Penny. You have many great moments of love that will be more than enough to overcome your anxiety moments. Call this an exercise in gratitude, but it is more than that. It

is an exercise in remembering who you are. You are the sum moments of all your love, and it is easy to forget that in the turmoil of daily living; but make a habit of recalling your moments of love. MAKE A HABIT OF REMEMBERING THE LOVE THAT YOU ARE. That's my wish for you."

"I'm going to do that. Right now."

"Have a love-filled day, and don't worry; God's love will protect you. I PROMISE."

"You don't make promises lightly, do you Padre?"

"I do not."

"Thank you."

"You're welcome."

"Okay, until the next time..."

Ciao, and all my love,
Orest

36. *The Fear and Excitement of Writing Stories from the Heart*

Tuesday, February 4, 2014

Dear Padre,

It's been a little over a month since my last letter, and although I kept meaning to drop you a line I never did; I got caught up writing stories. Which is what I'd like to talk to you about this morning.

You told me in one of my spiritual healing sessions with you that I should write more from the heart, but I feared doing that because it was so close to home; but I have started a new book of short stories and that's exactly what I am doing.

I've written nine stories so far, and I don't mind telling you that I went into each of these stories with fear and excitement; fear, because it's terrifying going in blind, and excitement because of what I might find there. And I both love it and hate it. Which brings up the theme of my book of stories—*enantiodromia*.

Carl Jung says: "I use the term *enantiodromia* for the emergence of the unconscious opposite in the course of time." This speaks to the two sides of the human personality, the outer conscious side; and the inner, unconscious side. That seems to be the theme of my stories in one way or another, and writing them has been very satisfying so far.

I just finished my ninth story yesterday, called *Blue Jeans/Red Roses*; and it was very satisfying to write because it was healing for me. I resolved some inner stuff that had to be taken care of; which leads me to say something about the individuation process.

I think I made an incredible discovery writing these stories: the *enantiodromiac* life is nature's way of individuating the consciousness of life. In other words, we grow through the conflict of our own opposites. We create our own **shadow personality**, and the tension that our **shadow personality** causes our conscious personality individuates the self. What do you think, Padre? Am I onto something here?

I really think I am, and I may write a spiritual musing on *enantiodromia*. In fact, I have the strongest inclination to call my book of short stories *Enantiodromia*. What do you think? It would be an intriguing title, wouldn't it?

I'm about to start another story, but I'm hesitant to begin. May I call upon you for a short dialogue on my new creative endeavor?

"I'd be happy to assist you in your new writing endeavor. I believe it will be some of your best writing. It will certainly lead to your best writing, because it comes from a place that speaks for the soul and not the mind. That's what art is supposed to be about. When you write or create from the mind you are not bringing anything new into the world; you are only rehashing the same old stale energy of life. The new and fresh energy of life comes from the heart. From your own experiences. Do

not be afraid to write about your own experiences, as you have been doing in these stories. These stories are the culmination of all your efforts to bring together the world of mind and the world of soul, and the combination of the two results in some pretty amazing stories. They are in my view the best things that you have written."

"Even better than my novel *Healing with Padre Pio?*"

"Yes, despite the fact that your novel addressed some of the most important issues that we have to face in life. It was a different genre, and I believe every genre has its place; but the creative art of story-writing is the genre that speaks to man the best, because it speaks to the soul of human existence, the very fabric of life. When a writer taps into the soul of man with his stories, he addresses the very heart of human nature; and this is what you are doing with your new book of stories. Keep it up. I see nothing but good for you in these stories; and yes, by all means send some of these stories to magazines. You will be surprised what results."

"Are we going to get together again for another book?"

"Yes. Let's just leave it at that for now."

"Okay. Any parting words?'

"You have embarked upon a very exciting course with your book of stories. It will prove to be much more rewarding than you can imagine. Finish this book. Just trust your instincts and listen to all the little nudges. You are right to be afraid and excited. This is the nature

of the true process of creative writing. If you take the word trembling to be a good thing, than you are in the "fear and trembling" stage of your writing career; and you will write some incredible stories that will leave their mark. Now get to work."

"Okay. Until the next time..."

Ciao for now,
Your grateful companion in Spirit,
Orest

37. Back to Hemingway

Dear Padre,

I've gone back to Hemingway, the early years, his apprenticeship days when he started out to become a writer, trying to capture the spirit of the young man who would one day win the Nobel Prize for Literature, re-reading his moving memoir *A Moveable Feast*, his first short stories, and several biographies—*The Apprenticeship of Ernest Hemingway, The Early Years*, by Charles A. Fenton; *The True Gen, An Intimate Portrait by Those Who Knew Him*, by Denis Brian; *Running with the Bulls, My Years with the Hemingways*, by Valerie Hemingway; *Hemingway: The Writer as Artist*, by Carlos Baker; *Ernest Hemingway on Writing*, edited by Larry W. Philips; *Portrait of Hemingway*, by Lillian Ross; and *Papa Hemingway*, by A. E. Hotchner, which I'm still reading. And then I watched a few You Tube videos of Paula Mclain who wrote the novel *The Paris Wife*, the story of Hemingway's first wife Hadley Richardson, which I have to purchase because it has piqued my curiosity; and I also have to purchase the biography of Hadley Richardson called *Paris Without End: The True Story of Hemingway's First Wife*.

I was enamored of Hemingway in my high school days, and I wanted to become a writer like him; but my destiny was to become a seeker instead. So writing was never my first priority once I began my quest for my true self; but I always stoked the fires of my desire to write, and I wrote somewhat; but never with the passion that was needed to become the writer that I dreamt of being one day. Now, all these years later, I want to become that writer; that's why I have gone back to Hemingway, the man whose life inspired me to become a writer but which circumstances would not allow me to be. And I've been very moved by how Hemingway's life turned out—which he regrets, as he confesses in his memoir *A Moveable Feast*. Speaking of his first wife, Hadley Richardson—"When I saw my wife again standing by the tracks as the train came in by the piled logs at the station, I wished I had died before I loved anyone but her."

Life is about choices, as Hemingway clearly tells us; but that's not what happened to me. I didn't have a choice to become a writer or a seeker. I HAD to become a seeker after the experience I had one night that brutally shocked my conscience. I had to find out what happened to me. I had to know; that's why I vowed to find my true self or die trying. And now that I have found my true self, I want to become the writer that I wanted to be in my youth; that's why I've gone back to Hemingway.

Thanks for listening, Padre.
Ciao for now,
Orest

Saturday, March 1, 2014

38. *The Lion that Swallowed Hemingway*

Sunday, April 27, 2014

Dear Padre,

Well, here I am back again. I'll bet you've been wondering what I've been up to since my last letter; but of course you know that I've been working on my new book, *The Lion that Swallowed Hemingway,* and I'm happy to say that yesterday I brought it home. Just as you said to me when I brought *Healing with Padre Pio* to closure, "I am content and satisfied with what we have accomplished," so too do I feel content and satisfied with my new book; and I just wanted to drop you a line to thank you for all your prodding and nudging from the other side, because I know that many chapters came to me by way of an inspired thought that helped carry my book along.

To be quite honest, I didn't know if I could pull this book off; but something magical happened in the writing of this book: it was teleologically driven. The seed of my literary memoir sprouted when I saw the television movie *Hemingway and Gellhorn,* which inspired me to go back to Hemingway, and I began to write a book of short stories; but after my tenth story ("An Angry Man in Georgian Bay") I was strongly nudged to write a memoir with my working title "Back to Hemingway."

My title changed after I wrote chapter seventeen, "The Lion that Swallowed Hemingway." Penny loved that title, and so did I; and then we went on the Internet and found a photograph of a lion with Mount Kilimanjaro in the background, and I had no choice but to call my book *The Lion that Swallowed Hemingway* because my favorite Hemingway story is "The Snows of Kilimanjaro." And yesterday I completed my last chapter, "Hemingway's Secret Way" and I feel a wonderful sense of completion, as though I could die today and feel like my life has been worth it.

I learned a lot writing this book. With all the research I did on Hemingway and re-reading his stories and novels I worked my way deep into the creative process, learning from my high school hero whose life and writing excited my imagination; and now that I've finished my literary memoir that delves into the life of Ernest Hemingway in a way that no biographer has done, I feel that I'm ready to take on creative writing with the knowledge that I needed to do my stories justice; and I have Hemingway to thank for that.

I learned a lot from the old master storyteller. He gave me insights into writing that I never knew, and they have inspired me to write with a new passion from the heart that I never wanted to tap into before because it scared the hell out of me. Hemingway gave me the courage to go deep into myself and "tell it as it was," to use his expression; and so, here I am, now that I have brought my new book to closure (of course, I have to work on the edit; but that's the fun part), I can go back to work on my new book of stories. So I just wanted to thank you for your contribution to my new book, which I know you helped me write because I felt your presence many times while I was working on it. In fact, I also felt the presence of the great writer himself, as well as C. G. Jung who plays a vital role in my new memoir. But hey, I need all the help I can get; don't I?

I do have to share one thing about this book with you, though. Very early in my new book I started to write what turned out to be the last chapter of the book: every time I tried to write that chapter which reveals Hemingway's secret way, I got steered in another direction; and it turned out to be my very last chapter! Was that you that steered me away?

I can feel you smiling at me, with the thought in my mind that it was Divine Spirit that was my guidance; and that's okay with me, because I know that you and Divine Spirit are one, and I want to thank you for your guidance because I just love the way my book ended!

That's all for today, Padre. I just wanted to let you know that I'm back on track again and can get to whatever needs to be done in my life. Writing can be such a demanding distraction from the daily duties of our life, but without this demanding distraction there would be no books to read, and where would we be then?

Until the next time,
Orest

39. *A Need to Talk with You*

Dear Padre,

I feel a need to talk with you this morning. Are you up to talking with me in that Jungian way that he called "active imagination."?

"Yes. You are in that place again that you always get to when you finish a new book, which by the way, is one of your best books yet. It is so informative on the way of life that you will be rewarded immeasurably by its publication."

"Do you have any advice on how to publish it?"

"Send out your inquiries and follow up with your own publication. See how that goes first. The natural law of synchronicity, which you call merciful and which I call the Love of God, will come into play the moment you send it out there. It is inevitable. The rewards for your publications are very subtle—not the big bang of instant appreciation by the reading public (that will come soon enough), but the energy that you receive from your books. They open doors that you cannot imagine; so just keep writing and self-publishing."

"So, what do I do now?"

"That's the question for today, isn't it? This is the early stages, the stage before the next seed sprouts, and it is not a pleasant place to be. It is very difficult to wait

for a seed to sprout; but the creative process is not unlike the garden of life: everything in its own time, its own season. You have learned much from your Hemingway book. It has cleared up a lot of issues for you (and the reader who has always been puzzled by Hemingway), and it has paved the way for greater insights into the journey to the total self."

"Padre, are you and I ever going to get to our next book together with the psychic who channeled you for our book *Healing with Padre Pio*?"

"Yes. And it will be wondrous!"

"I don't like where I am; but let's leave that for a moment. I want to share something with you. I'm reading Hemingway's novel *A Farewell to Arms*, almost half way through, and I'm taken aback. This novel does not compare to his short stories. They're much more rewarding. I honestly don't know what all the fuss was about this novel. As far as I'm concerned, it's not his best writing. In fact, I'm forcing myself to read it. But it does give me a greater insight into the man, because this novel is highly autobiographical; a fictional story of his relationship with the nurse Agnes that he fell in love with when he was in the hospital for his war wounds. Is it me, Padre; but do I see something about this man that other readers don't want to see?"

"Your knowledge of Ernest Hemingway is deep, due to your own understanding of the shadow side of the personality. You have given Hemingway the context that he needs to be understood. I'm surprised that no one has adopted this perspective on his life and work. You have

added a context that explains the complex nature of his personality, and your reading of his novels and stories is much more rewarding because of your insight into the man. This is why your literary memoir will be appreciated. Give it to the merciful law of God to work out, and it will find its place in the Hemingway cannon of studies. That is its destiny. That is why this book chose you to write it."

"Ha! So you do agree with me that the books choose the author to write them and not the other way around?"

"Yes, I do. The author must be ready to write it, of course. As you say, it is a two-way street. When the author is ready, his new book will choose him to write it. And now it is time for you to collect yourself and get on with your life. You must DO, DO, DO! That is your path to your total self. DO! In the doing, you overcome the staleness of life-fatigue. Doing generates the energy of living. Start with little things. Always the little things. Do not worry yourself about the big things. Do the little things, the smaller the better, because this is how you work up your confidence that is necessary for the bigger things, so don't hesitate whenever you are handed a little thing to do. DOING is your salvation—for today. What comes tomorrow will be what it may. So, DO!"

"I hear you. It doesn't matter what I do, as long as I do it. Don't get stuck between doing and not doing; that is HELL. Is that what you're trying to tell me?"

"Yes. Hell is not being what you are and being what you are not; it is that place between the two poles

152

of the enantiodromiac principle of life. It is what your teacher Gurdjieff would call 'standing between two chairs.' Sit on one or the other. Just DO, because in the doing the stasis is energized and the process of becoming (growing) is initiated. You have no idea of the power of DOING. It is the secret path to total self-realization. Okay?"

"Okay. Do, and trust; right?"

"That's the formula. Now put it to practice and let the Law of Love wash over you. I am happy for our little chat; now it is time to sign off."

"Right. Thank you for indulging me."

"You're welcome. One last thing. Do not feed your worries. Let them die of starvation. Catch yourself whenever you worry, and starve your worries to death. That's what I used to do. It's a discipline, but once you learn how to starve your worries you will be amazed at the extra energy you will have. Okay, now we can say ciao."

Ciao Padre,
Orest

40. *In Closing*

Dear Padre,

It's a strange, strange world; and the more I experience it, the stranger it seems to be. And to tell you the truth, I'm tired of all this strangeness. You told me in one of my spiritual healing sessions that I'm living my life over again in a parallel world, and as difficult as this was to believe at first it all makes sense to me today; and that's a strange place to be, because it's changed my view on everything.

I'm trying to work out this new perspective in my novel *The Golden Seed*, which I began writing a couple of years ago and have taken out to finish; and as much fun as it is to write, it kind of gives me the willies, because as exciting as it may be in its magical realism it cuts so close to home that it scares the normal out of me.

I don't know how I'm going to bring it to closure, which I know is going to happen soon; and all I can do is leave it up to my Muse to figure out. But to tell you the truth, Padre; I'm scared as hell and don't want to get back into it. But I have to.

I listened to the nudge to work on *The Golden Seed*, which interrupted the book of short stories that I was working on (*Enantiodromia and Other Stories*), and now I have to see it through; so I implore you, help me finish this story because I know that it will serve a vital purpose in this strange, strange world of ours.

Which brings me to something I've been meaning to bring up with you—what the hell is going on out there? I just don't understand this world any more. I don't have a clue where this world is headed, nor why people behave the way they do; and I'm wondering if the whole world has been hypnotized to behave so strangely. All I have to do is check the daily newsfeed on my Facebook page to witness how strange the world has become, and I can't for the life of me make sense of people anymore. What's going on, Padre? Is it me? Have I become too strange for this world?

Maybe that's what's happened. I don't know. All I know is that I don't understand where this world is headed, and instead of it making more sense to me with each passing year, it seems to be getting stranger. I'm sorry to bring this volume to closure on such a note, but that's how I feel. Maybe when I bring *The Golden Seed* to closure I'll feel different. But before I say goodbye, may I ask a personal favor?

I don't know how to put it into words, but I've been struggling for the longest time to get my life back in order, and I can't. I need help to assert myself to be myself so I can free myself from myself so I can be my happy self again, if you know what I mean; and I ask for your prayers to assist me in my journey of the self—

Until we talk again,
Ciao, my beloved companion,
Orest

♥

OTHER BOOKS BY OREST STOCCO

The Golden Seed

The Lion that Swallowed Hemingway

Do We Have An Immortal Soul?

Stupidity Is Not a Gift of God
Spiritual Musings – Volume 3

Tea with Grace
A Story of Synchronicity and Platonic Love

Letters to Padre Pio

Jesus Wears Dockers
The Gospel Conspiracy Story

Old Whore Life
Exploring the Shadow Side of Karma

Healing with Padre Pio

Why Bother?
The Riddle of the Good Samaritan

Just Going With the Flow
And Other Spiritual Musings

Keeper of the Flame

My Unborn Child

What Would I Say Today If I Were To Die Tomorrow?
Reflections on the Life of a Seeker

On the Wings of Habitat
A Volunteer's Story

About the Author

Orest Stocco was born in Panettieri, Calabria, Italy. He immigrated to Canada and studied philosophy at university. A student of Gurdjieff's teaching for many years which opened him up to the Way, his passion for writing inspired such works as *The Lion that Swallowed Hemingway* and *Healing with Padre Pio.* He lives in Georgian Bay, Ontario with his life mate Penny Lynn Cates. His personal dictum is: life is an individual journey.

Visit him at: http://ostocco.wix.com/ostocco

Spiritual Musings Blog:

http://www.spiritualmusingsbyoreststocco.blogspot.com

ME AND MY SISPHYEAN ROCK

www.ingramcontent.com/pod-product-compliance
Lightning Source LLC
Chambersburg PA
CBHW031846090426
42741CB00005B/370